DIVORCE IN ILLINOIS

The Legal Process, Your Rights, and What to Expect

Second Edition

Steven N. Peskind, Esq.

Addicus Books
Omaha, Nebraska

An Addicus Nonfiction Book

ISBN: 978-1-943886-86-9

Cover and typography by Jack Kusler

This book is not intended to serve as a substitute for an attorney. Nor is it the author's intent to give legal advice contrary to that of an attorney.

Library of Congress Cataloging-in-Publication Data

Names: Peskind, Steven N., author.

Title: Divorce in Illinois : the legal process, your rights, and what to expect / Steven N. Peskind, Esq.

Description: Second edition. | Omaha, Nebraska : Addicus Books, Inc., [2019] | Includes bibliographical references and index.

Identifiers: LCCN 2019011523 (print) | LCCN 2019012093 (ebook) | ISBN 9781950091102 (pdf) | ISBN 9781950091119 (epub) | ISBN 9781950091126 (kindle) | ISBN 9781943886869 (paperback)

Subjects: LCSH: Divorce—Law and legislation—Illinois— Miscellanea. | BISAC: LAW / Family Law / Divorce & Separation. | FAMILY & RELATIONSHIPS / Divorce & Separation.

Classification: LCC KFI1300 (ebook) | LCC KFI1300 .P47 2019 (print) | DDC 346.77301/66—dc23

LC record available at https://lccn.loc.gov/2019011523

Addicus Books, Inc.
P.O. Box 45327
Omaha, Nebraska 68145
AddicusBooks.com
Printed in the United States of America
10 9 8 7 6 5 4 3 2 1

To my clients past and present,
who inspire me daily to be the best lawyer possible.

Contents

Acknowledgments vii

Introduction ix

1 Understanding the Divorce Process 1

2 Coping with Stress during the Divorce Process . . . 22

3 Working with an Attorney 32

4 Attorney Fees and Costs 47

5 The Discovery Process 61

6 Mediation and Negotiation 74

7 Emergency: When You Fear Your Spouse 87

8 Parental Responsibility 95

9 Child Support 124

10 Maintenance 139

11 Property and Debt 151

12 Benefits: Insurance, Retirement, and Pensions . . . 170

13 Prenuptial and Postnuptial Agreements 182

14 Taxes 188

15 Going to Court 194

16 The Appeals Process 209

In Closing 215

Resources 217

Glossary 221

Index 231

About the Author 247

Acknowledgments

Few authors publish without the help of others. I am no exception. First, thanks to Rod Colvin from Addicus Books for giving me the opportunity to write this book. I appreciate his trust in me.

Thanks to all the lawyers, judges, writers, and academics who constantly seek to improve family law. No area of law influences so many, and, by extension, society at large. And thanks to all of my professional adversaries who make me a better lawyer.

My family always inspires. Much of my success comes from my wife Susan's encouragement and brilliance. My children and grandchildren keep me smiling and striving to go further. Undoubtedly, I am blessed by having them all in my life.

Introduction

What is a successful divorce? The expression seems contradictory. By definition, divorce suggests failure—anything but success. But the truth is that people survive divorce every day, and many have learned the secrets of the successful divorce. When you control your emotions and focus on the future in a positive way, you, too, may achieve a successful divorce. Life doesn't always turn out the way you want, but if you stay optimistic and focus on a positive future, you can survive most anything.

I have been practicing divorce law for more than thirty years. During that time, I have seen many divorce tragedies—people engaged in destructive behavior, irreparably hurting themselves and their children. But I have also seen many victories. I have witnessed courageous people who, despite being crushed and hurt to their very core, brush themselves off and start down a positive path to rebuild their future.

What are some of the mistakes I have seen? First, people invite disaster when they refuse emotional support. Many resources are available: counselors, life coaches, therapists, and physicians can all help you survive emotionally through this time. Those who refuse to get help often make poor choices, acting on emotion rather than reason. Recognize that this may be one of the most difficult periods in your life, and many people are there to help.

Lawyers have a vital role in helping you through the divorce process. Unfortunately, if you get the wrong lawyer, it may affect you the rest of your life. I have a friend who once told me that clients and their lawyers often resemble each other, not physically but temperamentally. Angry people hire angry lawyers, and smart people get smart lawyers. There may be some truth to this anecdote. Even if you are angry—and you may have a right to be angry—find a lawyer who will help moderate your emotions rather than mirror them.

Lawyers who jump at your command and don't discuss the consequences of poor decisions are not doing you a favor. Even though it may feel empowering to have a personal "attack dog," you will be left with the consequences of your poor choices long after that lawyer is gone. Find an emotionally mature lawyer who will help you make good decisions. This doesn't mean that you need to be passive and accept whatever your spouse throws at you. Don't be a victim! But choose your battles wisely with the help of a thoughtful and experienced divorce lawyer.

Similarly, don't look for a lawyer who will be your best friend. You probably have enough buddies, and your lawyer must maintain enough objectivity to evaluate your case critically. Emotionally, you may feel like you are in a sinking ship and you may want your lawyer to get into the boat with you, but if the lawyer does that, both of you will drown. The lawyer needs to stay dry, stand on the pier, and throw you a lifeline. Good lawyers balance advocacy with empathy and temper their actions with common sense. Don't ask your lawyer to give up his or her objectivity.

Knowledge is power. I hope this book will empower you. Divorce law is complex, and each divorce case is different; there is not a single right answer to every question. Further, divorce law is always in a state of flux, with new laws being passed regularly by the Illinois legislature. Divorce and family law are very fluid areas of law. Developments regularly occur. In fact, this second edition of *Divorce in Illinois* has been prepared to reflect all of the revolutionary developments in Illinois family law since the book was first published in 2014.

Because of this fact, I have created a page on my firm website that regularly posts significant updates to the law. Please visit (www.peskindlaw.com) and link to the page entitled "legal updates."

—Steven N. Peskind

1

Understanding the Divorce Process

At a time when your life may feel like it's in utter chaos, sometimes the smallest bit of predictability can bring a sense of comfort. The outcome of your divorce may be unknown, but there is one part of your divorce that does have some measure of predictability, and that is the divorce process itself.

Most divorces proceed in a step-by-step manner. Despite the uniqueness of your divorce, you can generally count on one phase of your divorce following the next. Sometimes just realizing you are completing stages and moving forward with your divorce can reassure you that the process will come to an end.

You may find that by developing a basic understanding of the divorce process, you won't be confused when your attorney starts talking about "depositions" or "going to trial." Such insights can reduce your frustration because you understand why each step is needed. It will support you to begin preparing for what comes next.

Most importantly, understanding the divorce process will make it easier to go through a divorce.

1.1   What steps are taken during the divorce process?

The divorce process in Illinois typically involves the steps listed on the following pages.

The Divorce Process

- Obtain a referral for a lawyer.

- Schedule an appointment with an attorney.

- Prepare questions and any reference material (such as tax returns) for the initial consultation.

- Interview multiple lawyers and find one who is a good fit for you and your case.

- Once you have chosen a lawyer, pay your retainer and sign a fee agreement. Determine, with the lawyer, what issues need to be addressed immediately.

- Provide requested information and documents to your lawyer. Take other actions as advised by your lawyer, such as opening or closing financial accounts, and cancelling joint credit cards.

- Lawyer prepares petition for dissolution of marriage and gets the case ready for filing. In some instances, the lawyer may reach out to your spouse directly to discuss the issues before filing a case.

- Assuming the case is to be filed, the lawyer files the petition with the clerk of the court. Assuming no safety concerns, and you are comfortable doing so, tell your spouse you filed for the divorce, and your lawyer will send the documents.

OR

- Sheriff or private process server delivers papers to spouse. Where necessary, the lawyer seeks emergency temporary restraining orders (without notice to your spouse) to restrain improper use of money or removal of the children from the state.

- Compete a financial affidavit, a financial disclosure form created by the Illinois Supreme Court.

- Lawyers negotiate interim matters such as temporary parenting issues, support, and temporary possession of the family home. If necessary, a court date is scheduled on those matters.

- Agree on temporary issues and the judge enters an agreed order.

OR

- The judge resolves temporary issues, either informally through a conference, or at an actual hearing.
- If there are minor children, parties comply with court rules and attend parent education class. If there is no agreement concerning the children, the parties must attend mediation and try to determine temporary and final parenting arrangements.
- Both sides conduct discovery to obtain information regarding all relevant facts.
- Value all assets, using expert opinions if necessary.
- Client confers with attorney to review facts, identify issues, assess strengths and weaknesses of the case, review strategy, and develop a proposal for settlement.
- Parties negotiate using written proposals, mediation, settlement conferences, or conferences with the judge.
- Parties reach agreement on all issues.
- Attorney prepares settlement agreement and all companion documents necessary to finalize the divorce.

OR

- If the parties cannot reach an agreement, the attorneys request a trial date.
- Trial preparations proceed, including preparation of witnesses, compiling exhibits, legal research on contested issues, pretrial motions, trial brief, preparation of direct and cross-examination of witnesses, preparation of opening statement, subpoena of witnesses, closing argument, and suggestions to the court.
- Trial
- Judge makes decision and enters a judgment for dissolution.

OR

- Attorney prepares judgment based upon court ruling.

- Decree is submitted to judge for signature.
- Judge signs judgment of dissolution. Prepare and sign documents (deeds or titles) according to the decree.

1.2   Must I have an attorney to get a divorce in Illinois?

You are not required to have an attorney to obtain a divorce in Illinois. A person proceeding without a lawyer is acting *pro se* (pronounced pro-say). Although permissible, representing yourself is rarely advisable if your case involves children, maintenance, significant property, or debts. If you are considering going it alone, you should at least consult with an attorney to discuss your rights and duties under the law. Undoubtedly, you will benefit from the opportunity to learn about the process and its pitfalls. Meeting with a lawyer can also help you decide whether to proceed on your own.

Some people cannot afford a lawyer, and others choose not to use a lawyer as a way to save money. Today, many people are empowered by information found on the Internet. But, a lawyer is more than merely an information bank. Good lawyers possess skills such as judgment, wisdom, and the ability to help you make choices based upon your long-term interests. Good lawyers know not only the law, but the judge as well: what the judge likes and dislikes in the presentation of a case. Also, when you represent yourself, you are deprived of the ability to analyze your circumstances objectively and might make decisions based on emotion rather than reason. As Abraham Lincoln famously observed, "A lawyer who represents himself has a fool for a client." The same can be said about nonlawyers.

In order to help people conduct a simple divorce on their own, the Illinois legislature has created a *joint simplified dissolution procedure.* The statute can be found in the database of Illinois compiled statutes at (www.ilga.gov/legislation/ilcs/ilcs. asp). This statute provides a streamlined procedure for people with no children or assets to get a divorce. If you are interested in using the joint simplified dissolution procedure, contact the clerk of the court's office in the county where you live. The clerk's office has a brochure and other printed materials to help you proceed on your own.

1.3. What is the difference between a divorce and a *legal separation*?

People with marital problems sometimes consider a legal separation rather than a divorce because a separation seems less permanent, less drastic. Some look at a legal separation as "divorce-lite." If you and your spouse want to just separate or take a "time out" from each other, work out an informal agreement regarding payment of bills and child-related matters, and then just physically separate without going to court. A *legal separation* is a formal court proceeding with the costs and expenses that go along with any court case.

If you do file a petition for legal separation, the judge will enter orders for maintenance, support, and parental responsibility. If you both agree, you can also divide your assets.

Once the court enters a decree of legal separation, you are still married. You can file joint taxes as a married couple and may be eligible for health insurance and Social Security as any other spouse. If your spouse dies, you are considered a surviving spouse for the purposes of collecting surviving spouse benefits from retirement, inheritance, and probate laws generally. Any assets or debts that either of you acquire after the decree of legal separation remain your separate property or debt, in the event you later decide to divorce.

Today people rarely use legal separations. The procedure is temporary and provides no real closure of the relationship. Since you are legally married, even if legally separated, you will need to get a divorce if you want to remarry or later decide to end the marriage with finality.

A legal separation usually isn't appropriate for someone who wants to change the status of their marriage, but isn't ready to "pull the trigger" for the divorce. Separate and get a good counselor. Don't incur the unnecessary cost of the legal separation. If the marriage can't be salvaged through counseling, proceed with a divorce at that point.

1.4 I made a terrible mistake. Can I get an *annulment* instead of a divorce?

The procedure formerly known as an *annulment* is a now known as a *declaration of invalidity of marriage*. A marriage declared invalid is considered legally null and void; it is as though you were never married. To be eligible for this, you need to prove:

1. One of the parties lacked capacity to consent to the marriage due to mental incapacity.

2. One of the parties was drunk or lacked capacity to consent due to drugs.

3. One of the parties married under duress.

4. One of the parties was forced to marry (the proverbial "shotgun wedding").

5. The marriage was procured by fraud.

6. One of the parties lacked the physical capacity to have sexual intercourse at the time of the marriage and the other party was unaware of that incapacity.

7. One of the parties was sixteen or seventeen years old and didn't have the consent of his or her parent or guardian.

8. The marriage was prohibited (for example, a marriage might be illegal because one of the parties never divorced their former spouse).

For items (1) through (5) above, the petition to declare the marriage invalid must be filed within ninety days of the discovery of these circumstances. For item number (6) the petition must be filed within one year of the discovery. For item (7), the petition must be filed before the underage spouse may legally marry without consent. For item (8), if the marriage was illegal, the petition can be brought at any time prior to the death of one of the parties.

1.5 I have a civil union and want to dissolve it. How do I do that?

You end a civil union the same way as a divorce: the procedures are identical. To end a civil union, you file a *petition for dissolution of civil union* and proceed as you would if you were a married couple divorcing. The substantive law is the same as in a divorce. The court can enter orders dividing property, determining parental responsibility, and setting up support and maintenance.

1.6 Is Illinois a "no-fault" state or do I need grounds for a divorce?

Illinois law no longer requires (or allows) one to allege or prove fault to obtain a divorce. Now, one need only prove that "irreconcilable differences have caused the irretrievable breakdown of the marriage" and the court determines that efforts at reconciliation have failed or that future attempts at reconciliation would be impracticable and not in the best interest of the family.

If the couple is separated for at least six months, the divorce will automatically enter upon request. A separation of less than six months requires some proof of irreconcilable differences. Separation does not require living in separate homes; rather, separation refers to the emotional relationship. If you both consider the marriage dead at a given point, you are considered separated even though you continue to reside in the same home.

1.7 My spouse told me she will never "give" me a divorce. Can I get one in Illinois anyway?

Yes. Illinois does not require that your spouse agree to a divorce. A threat by your spouse to deny you a divorce is an idle threat. If you have been separated for at least six months, or you can prove the marriage is irretrievably broken down, you are eligible to divorce without your spouse's consent.

1.8 Do I have to get divorced in the same state I married in?

No. Regardless of where you were married, you may seek a divorce in Illinois subject to the residency requirements discussed below.

1.9 We just moved here: how long do I have to live in Illinois to get a divorce in Illinois?

You or your spouse must be a resident of Illinois for at least ninety days to divorce here. The ninety-day period applies to the date the final judgment is entered, so, theoretically, you could move to Illinois tomorrow, file a case, and seek temporary court orders. However, the court can't enter the divorce decree until you have lived here for the ninety-day period. This ninety-day rule also applies if you are in the armed forces and stationed in Illinois for at least ninety days.

1.10 Can I divorce my spouse in Illinois if he or she lives in another state?

Provided you meet the residency requirements for living in Illinois (ninety days), you can file for divorce even if your spouse lives in another state. The court has the power to grant a divorce regardless of the presence of your spouse. However, before the court can enter any orders for support or divide property, it will need to obtain *personal jurisdiction* over your spouse. This means that your spouse needs sufficient contacts with the state to enable an Illinois court to enter any orders affecting his or her rights.

For example, if your spouse lived here with you and recently moved to another state, the Illinois court would likely determine there are sufficient contacts to enter orders here. Or if your spouse owns property here, the Illinois court would likely assume jurisdiction over your spouse and the case. Assuming Illinois courts can properly obtain personal jurisdiction over the absent spouse, the court can enter any necessary orders or judgments, just as though your spouse lived in Illinois.

1.11 How can I divorce my spouse when I don't know where he or she lives now?

Illinois law potentially allows you to divorce even if you do not know the current address of your spouse. First, attempt to locate your spouse. Contact family members, friends, former coworkers, or anyone else who might know your spouse's whereabouts. Use the Internet and any other resource available.

If you can't find your spouse, you may publish notice of the divorce in a newspaper. This procedure involves the clerk of the court running an ad in a local newspaper for several consecutive weeks, notifying the public of your intent to proceed with the divorce. Whether your spouse actually sees the ad is immaterial; the notice requirement is met by publishing in the county where the case is filed. The judge may then grant the divorce without more notice. Although this process does not confer personal jurisdiction over your spouse, it may allow the judge to grant a decree of divorce. Although the judge may grant your divorce by this form of notice, you may not get other court orders such as child support or maintenance orders by this method. Talk to your attorney about your options and rights if you don't know where your spouse is living.

1.12 I just moved to a different county within Illinois. Do I have to file in the county where my spouse lives?

You may file your divorce complaint either in the county where you reside or in the county where your spouse resides.

1.13 I immigrated to Illinois. Will my immigration status stop me from getting a divorce?

If you meet the residency requirements for divorce in Illinois, you can get a divorce here notwithstanding your immigration status. Talk to your immigration lawyer about the likelihood of a divorce impacting your rights.

If you are a victim of domestic violence, tell your lawyer. The federal *Violence Against Women Act* provides protection for abuse survivors, including both documented and undocumented immigrants.

1.14 I want to get divorced in my tribal court. What do I need to know?

Each tribal court has its own laws governing divorce. Requirements for residency, grounds for divorce, and the laws regarding property, alimony, and children can vary substantially from state law. Some tribes have very different laws governing the grounds for your divorce, removal of children from the home, and cohabitation.

Contact an attorney knowledgeable about the tribal court law for legal advice on pursuing a divorce in your tribal court or on the requirements for recording a divorce obtained in state court with the clerk of the tribal court.

1.15 Is there a waiting period for a divorce in Illinois?

No. Illinois has no waiting period for a divorce. You can begin a divorce immediately, subject only to the ninety-day residency requirement before finalizing the case. If you and your spouse are both residents of Illinois for more than ninety days, and you both agree, you can finalize your divorce within days of filing the case.

1.16   What's the first step in filing a divorce?

Have your lawyer prepare a *petition for dissolution of marriage.* This document, known as a *pleading,* initiates the divorce. The petition for dissolution of marriage is signed by the person filing for divorce, and filed with the clerk of the court in the county where you or your spouse lives. The petition will set forth basic background information, grounds for the divorce, and an inventory of what you are asking the judge to do. For example, the petition might ask the judge to enter an order regarding parental responsibility, support, or property division. The petition for dissolution is usually very short and does not detail all of your matrimonial difficulties.

1.17   My spouse said she filed for divorce last week, but my lawyer says there's nothing on file at the courthouse. What does it mean to "file for divorce?"

When lawyers use the term *filing* they are ordinarily referring to filing a legal document, such as a petition for dissolution with the clerk of the court. Today, all filings are done electronically. Sometimes a person who has hired a lawyer to begin a divorce action uses the phrase "I've filed for divorce," although no papers have been digitally filed yet with the clerk of the court to start the legal process.

1.18   If we both want a divorce, does it matter who files?

It depends. The judge is unconcerned with who files first; it makes no difference whether you are the *petitioner* (the party who files the petition initiating the divorce) or the *respondent* (the other spouse). In other respects, being the first to file could matter. For example, if you and your spouse live in different counties, the first person to file can choose where the case will take place.

Your attorney may advise you to file first or to wait until your spouse files, depending upon the overall strategy for your case and your circumstances. For example, if there is a concern that your spouse will transfer assets upon learning about your plans for divorce, your attorney might advise you to file immediately and also seek a temporary restraining order to protect against such an action. However, if you are physically separated from your spouse but have a beneficial financial arrangement, your attorney may advise you to wait for your spouse to file.

1.19 I don't want to embarrass my spouse by having the sheriff serve him or her at work. Is there a way to avoid this?

You can decide the preferred location to serve your spouse. You can have your spouse served anywhere he or she can be found: home, at the gym, or anyplace he or she frequents. Also, you can use a private process server, rather than the sheriff, who is more flexible with times and locations of service of process.

Talk to your lawyer about the option of having your spouse sign a document known as an *appearance*. An appearance is a document that voluntarily submits your spouse to the power of the court. If your spouse signs this document, you eliminate the need to have him or her served. Beware though; this procedure is not always appropriate. If, for example, your spouse doesn't follow up and file the appearance, you can't go to court and ask the judge for anything. If you have an emergency and need to get into court quickly, this may be a problem. Talk to your lawyer about coordinating with the sheriff or process server to ensure that service is done at the appropriate place and time.

1.20 Should I sign an appearance even if I don't agree with what my spouse has written in the complaint for divorce?

Signing the appearance does not mean you agree with anything your spouse stated in the petition for dissolution of marriage or anything that your spouse asks for in the divorce. Signing the appearance only submits you to the power of the court and avoids having the sheriff need to personally serve you with the documents. You do not waive any rights. If you do enter your appearance, you allow the judge to enter any appropriate orders related to the divorce. But if you sign the appearance and then take no action, the court will be able to enter a default order after thirty days. If you sign the appearance, you will be responsible for following all court rules.

1.21 Should I contact an attorney right away if I have received divorce papers?

If your spouse has filed for divorce, it is important that you obtain legal advice as soon as possible. Even if you and your spouse are getting along, independent legal advice can help you make decisions regarding your long-term rights.

After your spouse has filed for divorce, he or she can schedule a temporary hearing at any time. It is possible you will receive only a few days' notice of a *temporary hearing.* You will be better prepared for a temporary hearing if you have already retained an attorney.

After your appearance has been filed with the court, or the sheriff or process server has served you the papers, you must file a written response to your spouse's divorce complaint within thirty days.

1.22 What is an *ex parte court order*?

An *ex parte court order* is obtained by one party without advance notice to the other side. With the exception of temporary restraining orders and emergency orders of protection, judges won't sign *ex parte* orders. Ordinarily, the judge requires the other side to have notice of any requests for court orders.

When an *ex parte* order is granted, the party who did not request the order will have a chance to argue the propriety of the order during a subsequent hearing. At that time, the judge determines whether the *ex parte* order should remain in effect.

1.23 What is a *motion*?

A *motion* is a request for the judge to enter a court order of some type. For example, your attorney may file a written motion asking the court for temporary parenting time and decision-making rights and child support.

Some motions address procedural aspects of your case. For example, a motion to continue asks the judge to reschedule a court date. In some cases a motion may be made orally rather than in writing. For example, when an issue arises during a court hearing or trial, an attorney could make an oral motion requesting something from the judge.

1.24   Once my petition for dissolution is filed, how soon can a temporary hearing be held to decide what happens with our child and our finances while the divorce is pending?

In most cases, a temporary hearing can be held within weeks of filing and serving your spouse with the petition for dissolution of marriage, assuming you can give your spouse proper notice.

1.25   How much notice will I get if my spouse seeks a temporary order?

Each county has its own rules concerning notice requirements, but in most counties the notice can be as short as a few days. Frequently, in nonemergency situations, judges give the opposing party an opportunity to file a response to the motion, which will set the hearing date back by a few weeks.

1.26   What issues can the judge decide at a temporary hearing?

A variety of temporary relief is available while the case is pending:

- An order granting temporary child support or maintenance
- An order granting interim attorney fees
- An order allocating parenting time or decision making
- An order to preserve the status quo (prohibiting someone from selling something, for example)
- A restraining order or injunction prohibiting financial impropriety
- An order allocating time or responsibility with a companion pet
- An order granting exclusive use of the marital residence

These are just a few examples of the court's power to manage the couple's assets and behavior during the case. Consult with your attorney to determine if any requested court relief is necessary or permissible.

1.27 During my divorce, what am I responsible for doing?

Your attorney will explain what actions you should take, but consider the following:

- Keep in regular contact with your attorney. Get a new password-protected e-mail address to communicate with the attorney. Make sure you check your e-mail daily.

- Update your attorney regarding any changes in your contact information, such as address, phone numbers, and e-mail address.

- Avoid any major decisions (like selling an asset or moving in with a boyfriend or girlfriend) without first advising your attorney.

- Provide your attorney with all requested documents and information promptly.

- Complete forms and questionnaires. Confirm with your attorney any deadlines for completion.

- Appear in court on time and dressed appropriately.

- Be direct about asking any questions; you are not bothering your attorney if you have a question.

- Tell your attorney your thoughts on settlement or what you would like the judge to order in your case.

- Remain respectful toward your spouse throughout the process.

- Be respectful to your attorney and his or her staff (we all have crabby days but they are there to help; don't take out your frustration on them).

- Scrupulously comply with any temporary court orders, such as restraining or support orders. Notify your attorney immediately if you are unable to comply with the order.

- Advise your attorney of any significant developments in your life or your case.

By doing your part, you enable your attorney to partner with you for a better outcome while also lowering your attorney fees. If you don't cooperate with your attorney, he or she may fire you as a client, causing you the expense and inconvenience of starting over with another attorney.

1.28 I'm worried that I won't remember to ask my lawyer about all of the issues in my case. How can I be sure I don't miss anything?

Write down all of the topics you want to discuss with your attorney, including what your goals are for the outcome of the divorce. The sooner you have clarity in your mind, the easier it will be for your attorney to help you get what you want. Realize that your attorney will think of some issues that you may not consider. Below is a divorce issues checklist summarizing common issues in Illinois divorce cases.

Divorce Issues Checklist

Issue	Notes
Dissolution of marriage	
Allocation of time and decision making for minor children	
Possible relocation of children	
Parenting schedule (regular and holidays)	
Child support	
Extraordinary expenses (extracurricular, public school fees)	
Children as tax exemptions	
Life insurance to secure child support	
Child-care expenses	
Health insurance on minor children	
Private school or extracurricular costs for children	
College expenses for children	
Health insurance for the parties	

Divorce Issues Checklist (Continued)

Issue	Notes
Real property: marital residence (sale, refinance, postdivorce ownership)	
Real property: rentals, cabins, commercial property, (sale, refinance, postdivorce ownership)	
Marital expenses associated with real estate	
Time-shares	
Retirement plans (401(k), simple IRA, pension) ,QDROs	
Federal or military pensions	
Division of business interests	
Division of bank accounts	
Divisions of investments	
Division of stock options or RSU benefits	
Premarital or nonmarital debts	
Maintenance	
Pets	
Personal property division: including motor vehicles, recreational vehicles, campers, airplanes, collections, furniture, electronics, tools, household goods	
Exchange date for personal property	
Division of marital debt	
Claims of dissipations of assets	
Life insurance to secure maintenance	
Past-due sums owed under temporary order	
Tax indemnities for joint returns filed	
IRS Form 8332 for claiming children as exemptions	
Filing status for tax returns for last/current year	

Divorce Issues Checklist (Continued)

Issue	Notes
Restoration of former name	
Attorney fees	

1.29 My spouse has all of our financial information. How will I be able to prepare for negotiations and trial if I don't know the facts or have the documents?

After your divorce has been filed, your attorney will proceed with a process known as *discovery*. Through discovery, your attorney can ask your spouse to provide documents and information needed to prepare your case. Also, in many counties, the rules provide that at the start of the case, both parties must exchange information about their income, expenses, assets, and debts.

1.30 My spouse and I both want our divorce to be amicable. How can we keep it that way?

An amicable divorce is not always possible, but all should strive for one. An amicable divorce will not only make your lives easier and save you money in attorney fees, but will result in a more satisfactory outcome for both of you. Lower-conflict divorce will help you transition more easily after the divorce.

Find a lawyer who understands your goal to reach settlement and encourage your spouse to do the same. Some lawyers are incapable of compromise, so when you research potential attorneys, try to determine whether a particular attorney can work cooperatively with the other side. Personal references from former clients are always the most insightful. Lawyers who can't compromise are not likely to help you settle your case amicably.

Be proactive: compile and provide all necessary information to your lawyer and urge your spouse to do the same. Then ask your attorney about the options of mediation and negotiation for reaching an agreement. Even if you are not able to settle all of the issues in your divorce, these actions can increase the likelihood of agreement on many of the terms of your divorce.

1.31   Can I ask for a different judge?

Talk to your attorney about the reasons you want a different judge. If you believe that your judge has a conflict of interest, such as being a close friend of your spouse, you may have a basis for asking to substitute the judge. In that case, the judge will likely voluntarily step aside. Illinois allows a one-time change of judge without any cause or reason. You could change the judge simply because you don't like the color of his or her eyes. But be careful: as an unintended consequence, if you change your judge, you may end up with one who is worse for your case than the original assigned judge. And once you exercise your one-time right to change judges, you can't do it again and you will have to keep the new judge unless you can prove actual bias against you (which is very difficult to do!)

1.32   My lawyer keeps talking about what the judge will do, but I have told my attorney I want to settle the case. If we settle, isn't it irrelevant what the judge will do?

Yes and no. Obviously, if you and your spouse reach an agreement, the judge doesn't decide the issue. But the judge will still need to approve the agreement and if it is too unorthodox or unreasonable, the judge has the power to reject the agreement. Also, when negotiating, it is important to have some idea how the judge might ultimately look at the issue.

As a general rule of thumb, a good settlement gets you at least what the judge would give you if you went to trial, considering the fees and costs to get there. A bad settlement is less than you could get from the judge. Knowing what the judge might do is helpful to guide the settlement discussions. But there are more considerations than the amount of money you get. Often, the peace of mind and closure of getting an agreement outweigh the benefits of getting more money from a judge.

1.33   How long will it take to get my divorce?

The sooner you and your spouse agree, the faster your divorce will conclude. Generally, from the point that a full agreement is reached, it takes thirty to sixty days to finalize the divorce. In the absence of an agreement, cases may last many months and sometime in excess of a year depending upon the complexity of the issues or the court's schedule. The Illinois Supreme Court Rules mandate that all cases involving parenting issues conclude within eighteen months, unless there are extenuating circumstances.

1.34 What is a *marital settlement agreement*?

A *marital settlement agreement* is a contract that covers topics such as property division, maintenance, child support, attorney fees, and all other matters related to the divorce. Since the agreement may include legal terms unfamiliar to you, be sure to review this agreement with your attorney to make sure you understand all of its terms.

1.35 What happens after we reach our agreement?

After you and your spouse reach an agreement, settlement documents are prepared and approved by both parties and their attorneys. Those documents may include the following:

- A marital settlement agreement
- A written parenting plan
- A judgment for dissolution of marriage (the divorce decree)
- Qualified domestic relations orders (a QDRO is an order dividing interests in retirement benefits)
- Child support withholding orders
- Any other administrative forms or orders required by local rules

In addition, the attorneys prepare other documents to implement the agreement. For example, if one of the parties is keeping the house, the other spouse will need to sign a *quit-claim deed*. Ideally, all such documents should be prepared at the time the case is concluded.

After the agreements are reviewed and approved by the parties and the attorneys, the case is scheduled for a *prove-up hearing* before the judge. The prove-up is a short hearing that allows the judge an opportunity to review the terms of the agreement. The judge must determine that the agreement is not "unconscionable." An unconscionable agreement is one that is outrageous or oppressive. Even if you reach agreement, the judge has the power to veto any agreements that are oppressive or one-sided. In the event the judge determines that the agreement is unconscionable, you will need to keep negotiating to come up with agreeable terms that satisfy that judge. Depending upon local custom and practice, one or both of the parties must appear at the prove-up hearing and testify. The attorney(s) will ask questions about whether the parties fully understand all of the terms of the agreement. The judge will also want to make sure the parties entered into the agreement freely and voluntarily. Assuming the judge approves the agreement after the prove-up hearing, the divorce is concluded and the judge will then sign the judgment for dissolution, finalizing the case.

1.36   What is the significance of my divorce being final?

Once it is final, you are officially divorced. The entry of your divorce decree, known as the *judgment of dissolution of marriage,* is important for many reasons. This affects your right to remarry, your eligibility for health insurance from your former spouse, and your filing status for income taxes.

1.37   When does my divorce become final?

Your divorce becomes final on the date that the judge signs the divorce judgment. In most cases, this will be the day of your prove-up hearing. If you have a trial, the judgment is signed shortly after the judge has issued a ruling. Many people mistakenly believe that a divorce is final thirty days from the date the judge signs the judgment. This is not true in Illinois; it is final and fully effective the day that the judge signs it. Although either spouse can seek to reopen the divorce more easily during the first thirty days following the entry of the judgment, it is a final and enforceable order on the day the judge signs the final judgment for dissolution of marriage.

1.38   Can I start using my former name right away and how do I get my name legally restored?

If the court permits you to legally resume use of your maiden or former name in the final judgment, you may start doing so immediately. If you want your former name restored, let your attorney know so that this provision can be included in your divorce judgment. If you do resume use of your maiden name, take a certified copy of your divorce decree to the driver's license bureau to change your driver's license, to the Secretary of State's office to update your Social Security profile, and notify any other necessary persons of the name change.

2

Coping with Stress during the Divorce Process

During the divorce, your emotions may run from one extreme to another. Some days you may feel relief and ready to move on with your life. On others, you may feel painful emotions: anger, fear, or sadness. You may also feel a deep sense of loss or failure. Roller coaster emotions are a normal response to the end of your marriage. Remember, it is important to find support for coping with all these strong emotions. Because divorce is an emotional time, having a clear understanding of the divorce process and what to expect will help you make better decisions. And, when it comes to decision making, clarify your goals so that you can plan for a new and hopefully successful future.

2.1 My spouse left home weeks ago. I don't want a divorce because I feel our marriage can be saved. Should I still see an attorney?

A consultation with an attorney is the first step in any divorce. Understandably, if you don't want a divorce, you may choose to avoid this meeting. But avoidance is rarely the solution. Whether you want a divorce or not, your spouse may file for divorce. You may need to take action to protect your assets, credit, home, children, and future right to support. Hope for the best, but plan for the worst. Know your rights and be prepared, even if you decide not to file for a divorce at this time.

2.2 The thought of going to a lawyer's office literally makes me sick. I canceled the first appointment because I just couldn't do it. What should I do?

People frequently cancel appointments because of "cold feet." This is common and the attorney understands your reticence. Don't be embarrassed to call back when you are ready.

For many people, contact with a divorce lawyer is their first contact with any lawyer; anxiety is understandable. Ask a friend or family member to go with you. He or she can support you by writing down your questions in advance, by taking notes for you during the meeting, and by helping you to remember what the lawyer said after the meeting is concluded. The information you receive will help reduce your anxiety.

2.3 There is some information my attorney needs, but I'm too embarrassed to discuss it. Must I tell the attorney?

Your attorney has an ethical duty to maintain confidentiality. Your lawyer is obligated to keep your disclosures private. Attorneys who practice divorce law are accustomed to hearing embarrassing and intimate information about families. Although it is deeply personal to you, it is unlikely that anything you reveal will shock your lawyer.

It may feel uncomfortable, but it is important that you disclose this information so your interests can be fully protected. If speaking directly about these facts still seems too hard, consider putting them in a letter. If you cannot trust your lawyer enough to share this information, you should consider hiring a different lawyer with whom you are more comfortable.

2.4 I'm unsure about how to tell our children about the divorce. What's the best way to tell them?

Your discussion with your children will depend upon their ages and maturity. Consider consulting with a therapist or psychologist to determine the best way to approach this delicate topic. When possible, both you and your spouse should tell the children about the divorce together so that the children can see a united front. If your spouse won't participate, do your best to communicate the fact of the divorce in a way that does not malign your spouse, even if he or she is blameworthy. For the sake of your children, do your best to control your emotions.

Children often blame themselves for their parents' divorce. Be sensitive and reassuring to them. Emphasize that the divorce is not their fault. In this instance, less is more; don't get into the nitty-gritty causes for the breakup. This information just hurts the children. Reassure the children that everything will be okay and that they will continue to see both parents regularly.

After the initial discussion, keep the door open by creating opportunities for them to talk about the divorce. Use these times to acknowledge their feelings and offer support. Always assure them that the divorce is not their fault and that they are still loved by both you and your spouse, regardless of the breakup. If necessary, you and your spouse should discuss having the children attend counseling to help them understand and cope with their emotions.

2.5   My youngest child seems very depressed about the divorce, the middle one is angry, and my teenager is skipping school. How can I cope?

A child's reaction to divorce can vary depending upon his or her age and other factors. Some may cry and beg for reconciliation, and others may behave badly. Regardless of how your children are reacting to the divorce, it is important that you reduce conflict with your spouse, be a consistent and nurturing parent, and make sure both of you remain involved with your children.

Support groups for children whose parents are divorcing are available at many schools and religious communities. A school counselor can also provide support. If more help is needed, confer with a therapist experienced in working with children.

2.6   I am so frustrated by my spouse's permissiveness with the children. Is there anything I can do to counter this?

Feelings of guilt, competition, or remorse sometimes lead a parent to spend parenting time in trips to the toy store or engaging in special activities. Other times, the conduct is manipulative and the parent indulges the child to win their favor. Whatever the motivation, overindulgent parents harm children and cause problems. It is hard to compete with Santa Claus!

Even though this behavior is infuriating, try not to react or compete. Shift your focus from the other parent's behavior to your own, and be the best parent you can be. Maintain a routine for family meals, bedtimes, chores, and homework. Children crave structure, even while arguing about it. Structure provides a sense of safety and security, and ultimately, children are drawn to it. Encourage family activities, as well as individual time with each child. For those parents who use permissive or indulgent parenting as a weapon, rest assured that judges see through this behavior and will disapprove.

There is no simple solution to the vexing problem of the Disneyland parent so you can only control yourself and know that you are doing what is best for the children in the long run.

2.7 Between requests for information from my spouse's lawyer and my own lawyer, I am totally overwhelmed. How do I keep up?

First, simply get started. Often, thinking about a task is worse than the job itself. There's an old saying, "If you have to eat a frog, don't spend too much time looking at it; it won't become more appetizing." Just take the first bite.

Second, break your task down into small parts. Perhaps one evening gather your tax returns and on the weekend work on your monthly living expenses.

Third, get help. Ask a friend or relative who loves numbers to come over for an evening with her calculator to help get you organized. Also, consider hiring a divorce coach, who is specially trained to help you organize and complete these tasks.

Finally, communicate with your lawyer. Your attorney or paralegal may be able to give you suggestions or other assistance. Ask for their help if you cannot complete the project due to feeling overwhelmed or other factors.

2.8   I am so depressed about my divorce that I'm having difficulty getting out of bed in the morning. What should I do?

See your doctor. Feelings of depression are common during a divorce. You also want to make sure that you identify any physical health concerns.

Although feelings of sadness are common, more serious depression means it's time to seek professional support. Your health and your ability to care for your children are both essential. Follow through on recommendations by your health-care professionals for therapy, medication, or other measures to improve your wellness.

2.9   I know I need help coping with the stress of the divorce, but I can't afford counseling. What can I do?

You are wise to recognize that divorce is a time for seeking support. You can explore a number of options, including:

- Meeting with a member of the clergy or lay chaplain

- Reading motivational books

- Joining a divorce support group; consider using social media for this task

- Turning to friends and family members

- Going to a therapist or divorce coach. If budget is a concern, contact a social service agency that offers counseling services on a sliding-fee scale.

If these options are not available, look again at your budget. You may see that counseling is important enough that you decide to find a way to increase your income or lower your expenses to afford this investment in your well-being.

2.10   I filed for divorce, but I still have loving feelings for my spouse. Does this mean I should stop my divorce?

Many people continue to care about their spouse after a divorce is filed and well after the case is concluded. Whether or not to proceed with a divorce is a deeply personal decision. Emotion impacts our thoughts, and often clouds our judgment. A counselor or divorce coach is an ideal resource to address this delicate question. Have you and your spouse participated in marriage counseling? Has your spouse refused to seek treatment for an addiction? Are you worried about the safety of you or your children if you remain in the marriage? Do the bad days outnumber the good ones? Can you envision yourself financially secure if you remain in this marriage? Is your spouse involved in another relationship?

The answers to these questions can help clarify the possibility of reconciliation. Talk to your therapist, coach, or spiritual advisor to help determine the right path for you.

2.11 Will my lawyer charge me for the time I spend talking to him or her about my feelings about my spouse and my divorce?

Yes. If you are paying your lawyer by the hour, expect to be charged for the time he or she spends talking with you. Relying on your lawyer as a counselor can become very expensive. It feels good to have an empathetic ear, but don't use your lawyer for that purpose. Most people don't have unlimited money, and fees are better spent using your lawyer as a legal advisor rather than a friend or therapist.

2.12 My lawyer doesn't seem to realize how difficult my divorce is for me. How can I get him to understand?

Everyone wants support and compassion from the professionals who help during a divorce. Speak frankly with your attorney about your concerns. Not unlike other professionals, some lawyers have a better bedside manner than others. Express your concerns candidly. Improving the communication will help your lawyer understand how best to support you, and will help clarify which discussions are best left for your therapist or a supportive friend.

Probably more of a concern than a disinterested lawyer may be a lawyer who is too interested, one who loses his or her objectivity as a result of personalizing your case. Attorney-client relationships become impaired when the lawyer becomes unduly emotionally involved; he or she loses the ability to evaluate things clearly. And many clients, by their pleas of victimhood, invite this type of emotional involvement by the attorney. A healthy objectivity must be maintained for the lawyer to be effective.

2.13   I've been told not to speak ill of my spouse in front of my child, but I know she's doing this all the time. Why can't I just speak the truth?

It can be devastating for your child to hear you badmouthing the other parent. What your child needs is permission to love both of you. The best way to support your child during this time is to encourage a positive relationship with the other parent, even when your spouse doesn't reciprocate and demonizes you. If this occurs, have the children speak with a counselor to help neutralize the damage of this totally inappropriate conduct. In some instances, your spouse's conduct may be so malignant that legal intervention is necessary to stop it.

Discuss your options with your lawyer. Also, be aware of the emotional trauma to children when their parents engage in petty bickering. Does it really matter that the kids are brought home fifteen minutes late? Will the world stop turning if your ex didn't forward a report card. Pick up the phone and call the school to get copies sent directly to your home. A person's frustration is usually not really about the fifteen minutes or the report cards—it's about loss of control. And the result can be perpetual passive-aggressive arguments. Stop it! Your children deserve better. Your children are entitled to a close and loving relationship with both of you. And if your spouse engages in this behavior, don't react. Deny the fire any oxygen. Sometimes it takes the patience of Gandhi, but your children deserve it. It is not the divorce that hurts children as much as the ongoing conflict. Be the bigger person.

2.14   Nobody in our family has been divorced and I feel really ashamed. Will my children feel the same way?

Divorce is common today, and your situation is not unique in the community at large. Instead of shrinking from the divorce, concentrate on the positive and don't dwell on the negative. Change how you see your family identity. The best way to help your children is to establish a sense of pride in their new family and to look forward to the future with a real sense of possibility. Your children will have an opportunity to witness you overcoming obstacles, demonstrating independence, and moving forward in your life, notwithstanding many challenges.

Through your self-respect and positive attitude, you can be a great role model and teacher.

2.15 I am terrified of having my *deposition* taken. My spouse's lawyer is very aggressive, and I'm afraid I'm going to say something that will hurt my case.

A *deposition* is an opportunity for your spouse's attorney to ask you questions while you are under oath. The deposition allows the attorney to gather information and to assess the type of witness you will be if the case proceeds to trial. Feeling anxious about your deposition is normal. Regardless of the personality of the lawyers, most depositions are uneventful. Stay calm and relaxed and answer the questions to the best of your ability.

Remember that your attorney will sit next to you at all times to support you. Ask to meet with your lawyer in advance to prepare for the deposition. If you are worried about certain potential questions, talk to your attorney about them. Review information about your finances. If you are well prepared, your confidence will also increase.

2.16 I am still very angry with my spouse. How can I be expected to sit in the same room during a settlement conference?

If you are angry with your spouse, consider postponing the conference for a later time. Also consider counseling to address your feelings of anger.

Ask your lawyer about *shuttle negotiations.* With this method of negotiating, you and your attorney remain in one room while your spouse and his or her attorney are in another. The attorneys move back and forth between rooms discussing settlement options and opportunities. This process avoids direct contact between you and your spouse.

By shifting your focus from your angry feelings to your goal of a settlement, it may be easier to proceed. Try to look forward, and not backward, throughout the process.

2.17   I'm afraid I can't make it through court without having an emotional breakdown. How do I prepare?

Going to divorce court can be an emotionally charged experience. Some of these ideas may help you through the process:

- Meet with your lawyer or the firm's support staff in advance of your court date to prepare you for court.

- Ask you lawyer whether there are any documents you should review in preparation for court, such as your deposition transcript.

- Visit the courtroom in advance to get comfortable with the surroundings.

- Ask your lawyer about having a support person with you on your court date.

- Ask yourself, "What is the worst thing that could happen?" and consider what options you would have if it did.

- Learn how to meditate, both for stress management as well as a means to control your emotions.

- Avoid excessive alcohol, eat healthfully, exercise, and have plenty of rest during the period of time leading up to the court date. Each of these will help you to prepare for the emotions of the day.

- Plan what you intend to wear in advance. Small preparations will lower your stress.

- Visualize the experience going well. Picture yourself sitting in the witness chair, giving clear, confident, and truthful answers to easy questions.

- Arrive early at the courthouse and make sure you have a plan for parking your car if you are not familiar with the area.

- Take slow, deep breaths. Breathing deeply will steady your voice, calm your nerves, and improve your focus.

By taking the above steps, you can ease your stress.

2.18   I am really confused. One minute I think I am doing the right thing and the next I think I am making a terrible mistake. What's going on?

Denial, transition, and acceptance are common passages for a person going through a divorce. One moment you might feel excited about your future and a few hours later you think your life is ruined.

Moving through these phases doesn't always happen in a predictable order. Feelings of anger or sadness may well up in you long after you thought you had moved on. Similarly, your mood might feel bright one day as you think about your future plans, even though you still miss your spouse.

Taking good care of yourself is essential during this period of your life. What you are going through requires a tremendous amount of energy. Allow yourself to experience your emotions, but also continue moving forward with your life. Take it a day at a time and remember that things will usually stabilize as time goes on.

3

Working with an Attorney

You can be sure of one thing during your divorce—you will be given plenty of advice. Well-intentioned neighbors, cousins, and complete strangers will gladly tell you war stories about their ex or about their sister who got divorced in Canada. Many will insist they know what you should do, even though they know nothing about the facts of your case or the law in Illinois.

There is one person whose advice will matter though: your lawyer. Your lawyer should be your trusted and supportive advocate at all times throughout your divorce. This is not to say that the attorney must mindlessly advocate. Rubber-stamping your occasional poor judgment does you no good, and can hurt your case. If you're making poor choices, the attorney should help you redirect. The attorney's job is not to tell you what you want to hear but what you need to hear.

The relationship should be collaborative—both you and your attorney should work together to ensure the best possible outcome. The divorce will affect your and your children's lives for years to come, and it is vital that you get the best attorney available. You will never regret taking the time and energy to choose the right one for you.

3.1   How do I choose the right attorney?

Find a law firm that concentrates its practice in the area of family law and contact the firm to set up a consultation. You wouldn't go to a brain surgeon to fix your knee, nor should you consult a real estate lawyer for your divorce. It is also important to consider a lawyer with some familiarity with the court system in the county where you live. Each county has unique rules and it helps to get insights from someone who understands the local rules and knows the local judges.

The best recommendations for lawyers come from people who have personal knowledge about the lawyer's experience and skill. See if the lawyer has testimonials from past clients. Other resources include the membership directory of the American Academy of Matrimonial Lawyers (www.aaml.org), an exclusive organization that only elects accomplished and experienced family lawyers as members. Also consult directories in the following organizations that feature lawyers recognized as exceptional by their peers:

- Best Lawyers (www.bestlawyers.com)
- Leading Lawyer Network (www.leadinglawyers.com)
- Super Lawyer (www.superlawyers.com/illinois)

The worst way to find a divorce lawyer is by looking in the yellow pages and calling the lawyer with the biggest ad or choosing the first law firm listed on an online search engine, such as Google. Likewise, choosing a lawyer solely because of a free consultation is dangerous. Your children's future and your personal financial security are at stake, and the information you get at a free consultation is worth what you pay for it—nothing! Do your homework and research the firms that you find online or are referred to.

Good lawyers value their time and their advice, and when they don't value it by giving it away, neither should you. Advice from a wise and experienced divorce lawyer at the beginning of the case may make the difference between engaging in a bitter and acrimonious divorce, making you and your spouse mortal enemies for life, versus a cooperative divorce that will protect your children and assets and allow a healthy post-divorce relationship.

3.2   Should I interview more than one attorney?

Yes. Every lawyer has different strengths, and it is important that you find the one that is right for you. Meeting with more than one attorney helps you see clearly who will best be able to help you reach your goals in the way you want. People work better or worse with different types of lawyers, and having an opportunity to interview several lawyers will help you determine the "best fit" for you and your case.

Changing lawyers in the middle of litigation can be stressful and costly. It is wise to invest energy at the outset in making the right choice.

3.3 I don't have much involved in my divorce. Do I still need an expensive and experienced divorce specialist?

Probably not. There are many good, less expensive general practitioners who can help you. Likewise, many successful divorce firms have younger associates at lower hourly rates, who are supervised by older and more-experienced lawyers. By hiring these younger lawyers, you get the best of both worlds—divorce expertise at a reasonable cost.

3.4 What are some things I should be wary of when interviewing a lawyer?

Despite the jokes in popular culture, most attorneys are ethical, competent, and caring people. But, unfortunately, there are also some untrustworthy or incompetent lawyers. Although the Illinois Supreme Court tries to monitor unethical or incompetent behavior, it can't police all of the lawyers in the state all of the time. Here are some things to be alert to when you consult with a lawyer:

- Lawyers who promise you a specific result. No lawyer can guarantee anything.

- Lawyers who tout themselves as being the best or tell you they never lose a case. Braggarts are usually unsure of their skills and should be avoided. Confident lawyers don't need to crow.

- Lawyers who don't listen. If they aren't listening to you during the consultation, they are not likely to pay attention to you during the case.

- Lawyers who flirt or otherwise make suggestive sexual comments. Although you may be flattered, don't be. Predatory behavior towards vulnerable people is not complimentary; it is dangerous. Ethically, lawyers may not sexually involve themselves with their clients.

34

- Lawyers appearing mentally or emotionally impaired. Don't have your consultation in a tavern and expect top-notch representation.

- Avoid any conflict of interests or situations where the lawyer may be beholden to your spouse.

- Does the lawyer take a week to call you back to schedule your consult? If the lawyer takes that long to schedule the initial consultation, what do you think will happen after you retain him or her?

- Look around the lawyer's office. Is it a complete mess? This may be a sign of organizational problems that might impact your case.

- Avoid lawyers who are social friends. Although this may seem counterintuitive, you will do both yourself and your lawyer friend a favor by not mixing business with pleasure.

- A lawyer who is angry, disinterested, or otherwise unpleasant. You will be spending a lot of time with your lawyer, and you will be miserable enough. You don't need your lawyer making you feel worse than you already do.

- Lawyers who have been disciplined by the Illinois Supreme Court Registration and Disciplinary Commission. If in doubt, check the Illinois Supreme Court website at (www.state.il.us/court) to confirm that the prospective lawyer's license is current and whether he or she has malpractice insurance.

Trust your instinct. If a little voice is telling you that this person might not be the one, listen to it! There are plenty of good lawyers available. Don't compromise your or your family's future with someone who is incompetent or unethical.

3.5 My spouse says we should use the same attorney for the divorce. Is this a good idea?

Even amicable divorcing couples have differing interests. Consequently, lawyers' ethical rules disallow them from representing both parties to a divorce. When parties negotiate their own agreement, it is not uncommon for one party to retain an attorney and for the other party not to do so. In such cases, the party with the attorney files the petition for dissolution, and prepares the marital settlement agreement. The party without the attorney should at least consult with a different lawyer to review the agreement on their behalf. Independent legal advice on matters such as taxes, retirement, and health insurance issues helps clarify the implications of your agreement.

Although you may trust your spouse and his or her lawyer, know your rights before signing off on any agreement that will affect you for the rest of your life. A judge will not likely let you come back and change the agreement later based upon a lack of knowledge of your legal rights at the time of the divorce.

3.6   My spouse confuses me by telling me my attorney is not doing the right thing. What should I do?

Trust but verify. This advice from the cold war applies to divorce cases. Although it is hard to believe that someone you once loved (and may still love) would deceive you, it happens. Let your attorney do his or her homework for you. Sometimes, scheming spouses will crawl inside your head and tell you things such as "your attorney is just trying to run up fees by doing discovery…don't you trust me?" The answer to that comment should be, "I trust my lawyer to look out for my interests, and if you have nothing to hide, the costs will not be that much." It's not uncommon for manipulative people to try to drive a wedge between you and your attorney. There is a reason your spouse does this; he or she knows—maybe better than you—that your lawyer will get to the bottom of things. It is your attorney who you should now trust, not someone who you are divorcing. Early on, if you don't trust your lawyer, get another one.

Many think they are smarter than the lawyers and the judge. Few are correct. And the law has evolved to protect people. For example, you can't sell your business to your brother for ten dollars to avoid giving your spouse half the proceeds from the sale. Nor can you quit your job to avoid paying support. (You can quit your job, but your support payments will be based upon your former income). Game players rarely succeed and usually receive a payback by an unhappy judge. Ironically, these people often end up with less money than if they had played by the rules.

3.7 What is an *initial consultation* with an attorney?

An *initial consultation* is an important meeting that sets the tone of the entire case. At this meeting the attorney will discuss the law as it applies to your case and give you an overview of the process. Even if you are not ready to file for divorce, a consultation will provide valuable information that helps you plan and better understand the process. Also, if you suspect your spouse is considering a divorce, a consultation is a valuable resource to understand the consequences if your spouse proceeds with a divorce. Consultations, when done properly, help you prepare emotionally, as well as legally, for your divorce. It's not an exaggeration to say that this might be one of the most important meetings of your entire life.

Ordinarily, you schedule a consultation by calling the lawyer's office and asking to set up an appointment. Some lawyers allow this contact to be made by e-mail as well. Ask the person who schedules the consult what documents you should take to your initial consultation. At a minimum have some basic information about the family finances. Tax returns are helpful if you have them. When scheduling, ask about the consultation fee and be prepared to pay it at the time of the consultation. Take a list of your questions to your first meeting. Here is a list of common subjects to discuss at your consultation:

- Ask for an overview of the process generally and the law pertaining to your unique circumstances.
- Discuss the likely outcome concerning your children, or, if that is unknown, how courts decide issues of parenting time and decision making.
- Ask about using mediators to help in the case.
- Ask about your rights or obligations concerning maintenance and how courts address both the amount and duration of maintenance payments.
- Ask about financial contributions for the children, including child support, medical expenses, extracurricular costs, college expenses.

- Ask how property, including retirement benefits, is divided.

- If there is a business, ask how the courts deal with valuing and distributing the family business.

- Ask about the expected fees and costs for the divorce.

- Find out how courts allocate responsibility for fees and costs between the spouses.

- Ask about the expected duration of the case.

- Ask the lawyer about his or her philosophy of conflict management. Does the lawyer negotiate or go straight to court on issues?

- Ask the lawyer about his or her experience with the issues in your case as well as his or her experience in the county where the case will be filed.

- Ask the lawyer about his or her courtroom experience in the event an agreed divorce cannot be accomplished.

- Find out about the lawyer's office procedures and whether other people in the firm will assist the lawyer and how.

These are just a few of the topics that should be covered during a consultation. Don't be afraid to take a list with you and make sure you gain full understanding of the process so you can make informed decisions.

3.8 Can the information I share at the consultation be disclosed against my wishes?

Ordinarily, information revealed in a consultation is *privileged*. This means that the information cannot be disclosed, except under certain extraordinary circumstances. But there is an exception. The Supreme Court Rules provide that if the lawyer informs a prospective client in advance that the information disclosed is not privileged, that lawyer may later disclose the information and even represent your spouse. Make sure you clarify in advance whether the consult will be confidential.

3.9 Can I take a friend or family member to my initial consultation?

Typically, you may take someone to the consult but make sure in advance it's okay with the attorney (some lawyers believe the presence of a third person may nullify the attorney-client privilege). Having someone present during your initial consultation can be a source of great support. You might ask your friend to take notes on your behalf so that you can focus on listening and asking questions. Remember that this is your consultation, however, and it is important that the attorney hears the facts directly from you. Never take your children to the consultation. If the children have important information, the consultation is not the time for them to share it.

3.10 What exactly will my attorney do to help me get a divorce?

Throughout the process, your attorney assists you in a number of different ways. Attorneys serve as legal counselors: they help you make good decisions at a time when you will be challenged making decisions. They act as advocates, asserting your position in negotiations and in court. They act as litigation tacticians, helping you positively position yourself in the case. And finally they act as technicians, drafting documents and making sure all court rules are obeyed.

Your attorney may perform any of the following tasks on your behalf:

- Assess the case to determine which court has jurisdiction to hear your divorce
- Develop a strategy about all aspects of your divorce, including the treatment of assets and matters concerning children and how best to assert arguments on your behalf
- Prepare legal documents for filing with the court
- Help you formulate a settlement stance and then negotiate on your behalf
- Act as a sounding board concerning the pros and cons of settlement offers

- Conduct discovery to obtain information from the other party, which could include depositions, requests for production of documents, and written interrogatories
- Assist in choosing appropriate experts to value your assets such as businesses or real estate
- Appear with you at court appearances, depositions, and conferences
- Schedule all deadlines and court appearances
- Support you in responding to information requests from your spouse
- Inform you of actions you are required to take
- Perform financial analyses of your case, including, when necessary, hiring experts to help find undisclosed assets or money
- Conduct legal research
- Prepare you for court appearances and depositions
- Prepare your case for hearings and trial, including choosing and preparing exhibits and witnesses
- Advise you regarding your rights under the law
- Counsel you regarding the risks and benefits of negotiated settlement as compared to proceeding to trial

As your advocate, your attorney is entrusted to take all of the steps necessary to represent your interests in the divorce.

3.11 What professionals might the court appoint to work with my attorney?

The Illinois Supreme Court Rules require that, prior to going to court, parties who cannot resolve issues of parental decision making and parenting time must attend *mediation* to try to resolve those issues. A *mediator* is a neutral third party who helps you and your spouse negotiate an agreement. The mediator does not act as a private "judge" and does not make decisions concerning the best interest of your children. Rather, the mediator helps you stay focused on the best interest of your children and keeps the discussions on track. The mediator is typically an attorney or therapist, and you and your spouse will be responsible for paying the mediator's fees.

When mediation is unsuccessful, courts often appoint a *guardian ad litem (GAL),* or child representative, who represents the best interest of the child. A guardian *ad litem* investigates and reports to the judge his or her opinions concerning the best interest of the children. The guardian *ad litem* may then be called as a witness at trial to testify about any relevant observations or his or her ultimate opinions.

A *child representative,* in contrast, investigates and advocates for the best interest of the child in court, but does not testify as a witness or give an opinion. The court may also appoint an attorney for the children, who will provide independent legal counsel for the children. Both the guardian *ad litem* and the child advocate are specially trained attorneys. The court will order the parties to pay the fees and costs of these professionals.

Another expert who could be appointed by the court is a psychologist or other trained mental health professional. The law allows the judge to call upon an expert to investigate the mental health or parenting strengths and weaknesses of both parents. The role of the psychologist will depend upon the purpose for which she or he was appointed. For example, the psychologist may be appointed to perform an evaluation, which involves assessing both parents and children and rendering an opinion regarding the best interest of the children. Or the expert may be ordered to evaluate one parent to assess the child's safety while spending time with that parent. The divorcing couple is also responsible for the costs of the court's expert.

Finally, the judge can appoint an independent financial expert to address financial issues or to value property or business interests. This expert is a resource for the judge, who is seeking information to help resolve a case. Both parties are responsible for the cost of this independent financial expert.

3.12 I've been divorced before, and I don't think I need an attorney this time; however, my spouse is hiring one. Is it wise to go it alone?

It is important to remember that every divorce is different. The length of the marriage, whether there are children, the relative financial situation for you and your spouse, as well as your age and health can all affect the financial outcome in your divorce. Also, the law may have changed since your last divorce. Some aspects of divorce law are likely to change each year. The legislature passes new laws and the appellate and Supreme Court continually decide cases that affect the rights and responsibilities of people who divorce.

In some cases, the involvement of your lawyer could be minimal. The law allows *limited-scope representation*, which allows a lawyer to perform certain limited services rather than formally appearing as your attorney for all phases of the case. This type of representation may be appropriate if there are few contested issues and the two of you remain amicable. At a minimum, consult with an attorney to discuss your rights and have an attorney review any final agreement.

3.13 Can I take my children to meetings with my attorney?

Make other arrangements for your children when you meet with your attorney. Your attorney will be giving you a great deal of important information during your conferences, and it will benefit you to give your full attention. The lawyer may not be able to speak freely with you if a child is present.

Keep information about the legal aspects of your divorce away from your children. Knowledge that you are seeing an attorney can add to your child's anxiety about the process. It can also make your child a target for questioning by the other parent about your contacts with your attorney.

Most law offices are not designed to accommodate young children and are ordinarily not "child-proof." For both your child's well-being and your own peace of mind, get a sitter when you have meetings with your attorney.

There may be occasions when you feel your child may have important information that you want the child to share with the attorney. Discuss this with the attorney before bringing the child to a meeting. The attorney may want the child to be interviewed by the guardian *ad litem* or child representative, or might prefer to have the child relate the information to some other professional. As a general rule, don't use your child as a resource; it harms the child and may impact the child's relationship with the other parent. Remember, when children are made soldiers in their parent's war, they are the first casualties.

3.14 What is the role of the *paralegal* or *legal assistant* in my attorney's office?

A *paralegal* or *legal assistant* is a trained legal professional who provides support for you and your lawyer. Working with paralegals helps lower your legal costs, because the hourly rate for paralegal services is less than the rate for attorneys.

Here are some examples of ways paralegals assist attorneys in divorce cases:

- Preparing routine documents for the attorney's review
- Helping to prepare discovery responses
- Interviewing witnesses to gather information
- Organizing, collating, and inventorying documents that are received in the case
- Working on financial affidavits
- Helping the lawyer prepare for trial
- Doing legal research
- Being a trial assistant, attending court dates to assist the lawyer during the hearing

It is important that you respect the limits of the paralegal's role. Although a paralegal can answer many questions and provide a great deal of information to you, he or she cannot give legal advice. Paralegals help you by analyzing your information, reviewing documents with you, providing you with updates on your case, and answering questions about the divorce process that do not call for legal advice.

Also, sometimes lawyers hire law students to serve as law clerks. Ordinarily, law clerks help attorneys by doing legal research or preparing pleadings. They act in a similar capacity to a paralegal.

3.15 My attorney is not returning my phone calls or e-mails. What can I do?

You have a right to expect responsiveness from your lawyer. Here are some options to consider when you cannot reach your lawyer:

- Ask to speak to the paralegal or another attorney in the office.

- Send an e-mail or fax telling your lawyer that you have been trying to reach him or her by phone and explaining the reason it is important that you receive a return call.

- Ask an assistant to schedule a phone conference for you to speak with your attorney at a specific date and time.

- Schedule a meeting with your attorney to discuss both the issue needing attention as well as your concerns about the communication.

Ordinarily, an attorney wants to provide good service to you. If your calls are not returned, it may mean that the attorney is involved in a complicated trial or otherwise unable to get back to you. But, in that instance, the lawyer's secretary, paralegal, or law clerk should call you back. Sometimes a law office must do triage. The assistant should determine your problem and consult with the lawyer to see if your problem needs immediate attention. Sometimes the issue can wait until the attorney gets a breather. The assistant should then call you back to discuss the game plan.

If your lawyer is always too busy to answer your questions, that suggests either poor time-management skills or disinterest in your case. In either event, this cannot be tolerated and you should consider hiring another lawyer.

3.16 How do I know when it's time to change lawyers?

Changing lawyers is costly. You will incur legal fees for your new attorney to review information that is already familiar to your current attorney. You will spend time giving much of the same information to your new lawyer that you already gave to the one you have discharged. Even though the case doesn't start over from the beginning, a change in lawyers often delays the divorce.

The following are questions to ask yourself when you're deciding whether to stay with your attorney or seek new counsel:

- Have I spoken directly to my attorney about my concerns?

- Am I constantly put off when I ask questions? Are the answers unsatisfactory?

- When I expressed concerns, did my lawyer take action?

- Am I part of the problem? Do I follow through when asked?

- Is my lawyer open and receptive to what I have to say?

- Am I blaming my lawyer for bad behavior by my spouse or opposing counsel?

- Have I provided my lawyer the information needed for taking the next action?

- Does my lawyer have control over the complaints I have, or does the law or the judge limit what my lawyer can do?

- Is my lawyer unwilling to fight for me when necessary?

- Conversely, is my lawyer unwilling to make even reasonable concessions?

- Are my phone calls returned? Are my questions answered reasonably promptly?

- Is my lawyer keeping promises for completing action on my case?

- Do I trust my lawyer?

- Am I getting large bills each month but nothing seems to be happening to advance the case?

- What would be the advantages of changing lawyers when compared to the cost?

- Do I believe my lawyer will support me to achieve the outcome I'm seeking in my divorce?

Every effort should be made to resolve concerns about your attorney. However, if you have made this effort and the situation remains unchanged, it may be time to switch lawyers.

4

Attorney Fees and Costs

The cost of your divorce might be one of your greatest concerns. Because of this, become an intelligent consumer of legal services. You want quality, but you also want to get the best value for the fees you are paying.

Legal fees for a divorce can be costly and the total expense not always predictable. But there are many actions you can take to control and estimate the cost. Develop a plan for how you will finance your divorce. Speak openly with your lawyer about fees from the outset. Learn as much as you can about how you will be charged. Insist on a written fee agreement.

By being informed, aware, and wise, your financial investment in your divorce will be money well spent to protect your future.

4.1   Can I get free legal advice from a lawyer over the phone?

Each firm treats calls from prospective clients differently. But most questions about your divorce are too complex for a lawyer to give a meaningful answer during a brief phone call.

Questions about your divorce require a complete look at the facts, circumstances, and background of your marriage. To obtain helpful legal advice, it's best to schedule an initial consultation with a lawyer who handles divorces.

4.2 Will I be charged for an initial consultation with a lawyer?

Some lawyers give free consultations, while others charge a fee. Those who offer free consultations usually do so as a business strategy. More-highly qualified lawyers charge a consult fee and provide more-personalized and in-depth analysis during the meeting. When scheduling your appointment, you should be told the amount of the fee.

4.3 Will I be expected to pay the attorney after our first meeting? If so, how much?

If your attorney charges for an initial consultation, be prepared to make payment at the time of your meeting. At the close of your consultation, the attorney may also tell you the amount of the retainer needed for the law firm to handle your divorce. However, you are not expected to pay the retainer at the time of your first meeting. Rather, the retainer is paid after you have decided to hire the lawyer, the lawyer has accepted your case, and you are ready to proceed.

4.4 What exactly is a *retainer* and how much will mine be?

A *retainer* is a sum paid to your lawyer in advance for services to be performed and costs to be incurred in your divorce. This will be either an amount paid toward a "flat fee" for your divorce or an advance for services that will be charged by the hour.

If the law firm accepts your case, expect the attorney to request a retainer following the initial consultation. The amount of the retainer depends upon the nature of your case. Contested parenting issues, and divorces involving businesses or interstate child relocation disputes are likely to require higher retainers. Other factors that can affect the amount of the retainer include the nature and number of the disputed issues, and the level of acrimony between you and your spouse.

The lawyer must provide periodic itemized statements reflecting use of the retainer. By law, the retainer is refundable if you decide not to proceed with the divorce or if you terminate the lawyer's services prior to exhausting the retainer.

4.5   I don't have any money and I need a divorce. What are my options?

Check into the availability of *pro bono services* through a local bar association or the clerk of the court in the county where you live. Pro bono services are free legal services available for those with little or no income. Another option is to do the divorce yourself, getting forms from a local law library or the clerk of the court. As mentioned earlier, you can also hire a lawyer under a limited-scope arrangement. Here, the lawyer's involvement is limited to certain agreed-upon tasks (drafting documents or consulting) and the lawyer doesn't assume responsibility for the whole case. This is a lower-cost alternative. Note that if you live near a law school, you may find that law students offer legal help at lower rates. Finally in some instances certain attorneys will accept the case and pursue your spouse for fees.

4.6   I don't have much money, but I need to get started. What should I do?

If you have some money and want to divorce as soon as possible, consider some of these options:

- Borrow the legal fees.
- Charge the legal fees on a credit card.
- Talk to an attorney about using money held in a joint account with your spouse.
- Find an attorney who will allow you to make installment payments.
- Find an attorney who will pursue your spouse for payment.

Even if you do not have the financial resources to proceed with your divorce at this time, consult with an attorney to learn your rights and to develop an action plan for steps you can take between now and the time you are able to proceed.

4.7   How much does it cost to get a divorce?

The cost of your divorce will depend upon many factors. Some attorneys perform divorces for a flat fee, but most charge by the hour. A *flat fee* is a fixed amount for the legal services provided. A flat fee is more likely to be used when you and your spouse have no children together and you have agreed upon all issues in the case. Most Illinois attorneys charge by the hour for divorces.

It is important that you discuss the cost of your divorce at your first meeting with your attorney. Although most attorneys cannot give you an exact estimate, many can give you a range of possible fees. Ask your attorney to provide such an estimate. But remember, there are a lot of moving parts in any divorce and it is virtually impossible to estimate the cost with any precision.

4.8   What are typical hourly rates for a divorce lawyer?

In Illinois, fees vary. Some divorce attorneys charge as low as $100 per hour. Others charge many multiples of that rate and fees exceed $500 per hour. The rate your attorney charges may depend upon factors such as the complexity of the issues, the attorney's skills, reputation, and experience; and what other attorneys in the community are charging.

If you have a concern about an individual attorney's hourly rate, but you would like to use that lawyer's firm, consider asking to work with an associate attorney in the firm who is likely to charge a lower rate. Associates ordinarily have less experience than the senior lawyers but are skilled divorce lawyers nevertheless. Usually these junior lawyers are trained and mentored by the more-experienced lawyers, and are fully capable of handling your case.

A higher hourly rate doesn't necessarily mean a higher total cost. Paying for a more-experienced attorney may actually result in a lower cost due to that lawyer's ability to anticipate and avoid costly problems. Also, a well-respected lawyer's inherent credibility with the opposing counsel and the judge often gets cases settled, avoiding costly hearings.

4.9   Can I make payments to my attorney rather than pay a retainer?

Every law firm has individual policies regarding payment arrangements for divorce clients. Often these arrangements are tailored to the specific client. Most attorneys will require a substantial retainer to be paid at the outset of your case. Some attorneys may accept monthly payments in lieu of the retainer. Others may require monthly payments, or request additional retainers as your case progresses. Don't be embarrassed to discuss the lawyer's expectations about fees. If the lawyer does not raise the issue during your initial meeting, make sure that you address it.

4.10 I agreed to pay my attorney a substantial retainer to begin my case. Will this be my total bill or will I need to make additional payments?

A retainer is a prepayment for services to be rendered. The services performed at the agreed-upon hourly rate are credited against the retainer. For example, assume the retainer is $5,000. In the first month, the attorney bills $500 for services. The lawyer has earned the $500 and you have a credit balance of $4,500. When that balance has been whittled down by the performance of future services, the lawyer will either ask for another prepayment retainer, a monthly payment, or agree to seek fees from your spouse. Some attorneys will agree to wait to be paid until the end of the case.

Ask your attorney for his or her expectations about ongoing payments on your account. Determine whether the lawyer expects monthly payments or payment in full, whether the firm will ask you to pay additional retainers, and whether the firm charges interest on past-due accounts. Regular payments to your attorney can help you avoid having an unexpected large legal bill at the end of your case.

4.11 My lawyer wants me to pay an *evergreen retainer.* What is that?

An *evergreen retainer* requires you to replenish the retainer automatically when it falls below a given amount. For example, assume the retainer is $10,000. The evergreen provision provides that you will ensure that the retainer never falls below $5,000 by paying any sums monthly to keep a balance in the account of at least $5,000.

4.12 My lawyer gave me an estimate of the cost of my divorce and it sounds reasonable. Do I still need a *written fee agreement*?

Absolutely. Insist upon a *written fee agreement* with your attorney. A fee agreement defines the scope of the services, and also outlines the attorney's hourly rate, whether you will be billed for copying costs, and when you can expect to receive statements on your account. A fee agreement reduces the risk of misunderstandings between you and your lawyer. It sets forth your mutual obligations and responsibilities so that you both can focus on the legal services rather than on disputes about fees.

By statute, all fee agreements for divorce-related services must contain a *Statement of Client's Rights and Responsibilities*. The language of this statement must be printed verbatim from the language in the statute, 750 ILCS 5/508(f). The statement discusses the client's rights, including the following:

- A specific outline of the scope of representation and the fees to be charges
- A right to competent representation
- Reasonable diligence by the attorney
- A right to confidentiality of information disclosed during the case
- Periodic updates about the status of the case
- Regular itemized billing statements, at least quarterly
- A right to the refund of the unused portion of the retainer

4.13 How will I know how the fees and charges are accumulating?

Be sure your written fee agreement describes how you will be informed about the status of your account. If your attorney agrees to handle your divorce for a flat fee, your fee agreement should clearly set forth what services are included in the fee.

Make sure your written fee agreement includes a provision for the attorney to provide regular statements of your account.

Even though the statute requires statements at least quarterly, it is reasonable to ask that these be provided monthly.

Review the statement of your account promptly after you receive it. Check to make sure there are no errors, such as duplicate billing entries. If your statement reflects work that you were unaware was performed, call for clarification. Your attorney's office should welcome any questions you have about services it provided. Your billing statement might also include filing fees, court reporter fees for transcripts of court testimony or depositions, copy expenses, or interest charged on your account.

If several weeks have passed and you have not received a statement on your account, call your attorney's office to request one. Legal fees can mount quickly, and it is important that you stay aware of the status of your account.

4.14 What other expenses are related to the divorce litigation besides lawyer fees?

Talk to your attorney about costs other than the attorney fees. Ask whether it is likely there will be filing fees, court reporter expenses, subpoenas, or expert-witness fees. Also, determine whether you will be charged for administrative costs, such as copy fees. Expert-witness fees can be a substantial expense, ranging from hundreds to thousands of dollars, depending upon the type of expert and the extent to which he or she is involved in your case.

Speak frankly with your attorney about these costs so that together you can make the best decisions about how to use your budget for the litigation.

4.15 Who pays for the experts such as appraiser, accountant, and psychologist?

The divorcing parties pay the costs of the experts, whether appointed by the court or privately hired. Since you will ultimately be responsible for the costs, make sure that your lawyer consults with you before retaining an expert. Expert fees can be expensive, depending upon the scope of the employment. Not unlike attorneys, "you get what you pay for" and a well-respected and competent expert can impact the results of your case. "Top-gun" experts are often a necessary investment for a successful result. Make sure you understand the expert's fees and try to get an estimate of the total cost before they commence work. Often, the expert will request that you sign a retainer agreement.

In the case of the guardian *ad litem,* who may be appointed to represent the best interest of your children, the amount of the fee will depend upon how much time this professional spends on your case. The judge often orders this fee to be shared by the parties. However, depending upon the circumstances, one party can be ordered to pay the entire fee.

Psychologists either charge by the hour or set a flat fee for certain evaluations. As with the guardian *ad litem,* the court can order one party to pay this fee or both parties to share the expense. It is not uncommon for a psychologist to request payment in advance and hold the release of an expert report until fees are paid.

The fees for business evaluators, appraisers, and accountants depend on the scope of the assignment and whether the expert will need to appear as a witness at a deposition or trial. Illinois law requires parties in a divorce trial to present testimony regarding the value of all assets. Unless you and your spouse can agree on values, you will need to present testimony, usually through experts, of the value of unusual assets such as businesses, collections, equipment, or real estate.

4.16 What factors will impact how much my divorce will cost?

Although your ultimate fee is difficult to predict, the following are some of the factors that affect the cost:

- Whether there are children
- Whether you and your spouse agree to parental responsibility and allocation of parenting time
- Whether domestic violence or child abuse is involved
- Whether there are novel legal questions
- Whether one or both of the parties file for bankruptcy
- Out-of-control emotions by either party
- The number of assets (larger estates involve more work to investigate and value)

- Complicated valuation issues, such as a business or other property
- The nature of the contested issues
- Gamesmanship (such as one party hiding assets or income)
- The cooperation of the opposing party and opposing counsel

4.17   Will my attorney charge for phone calls and e-mails?

Unless your case is handled on a flat-fee basis, expect to be billed for phone calls and e-mails with your lawyer. Much of the professional services are provided by phone and by e-mail. This time includes giving legal advice, negotiating, or gathering information to protect your interests. These calls and e-mails are all billable legal services.

To make the most of your time during these communications with your attorney, plan your call or e-mail in advance. Organize what you want to communicate, your questions, and any specific concerns. This will help you to be clear and focused so that your fees are well spent. Contact your attorney once with five questions rather than calling five times with five separate questions. By using your attorney's time efficiently, you will help keep your bill down.

4.18   Will I be charged for talking to my lawyer's staff?

Check the terms of your fee agreement. Any fees for non-lawyer staff should be spelled out in advance. Whether you are charged these fees may depend upon their role in the office. For example, many law firms charge for the services of paralegals and law clerks. Remember that nonlawyer staff members cannot give legal advice; respect their roles and their limitations. Don't ask receptionists and secretaries to give you an opinion regarding whether you will receive all parenting responsibility or receive maintenance.

Your lawyer's support staff will be able to relay your messages and receive information from you. They may also be able to answer many of your questions. Proper use of the lawyer's support staff will help the lawyer better manage the case and help you save fees as well.

4.19   What is a *litigation budget,* and how do I know if I need one?

If your case is complex and you are anticipating substantial legal fees, ask your attorney to prepare a *litigation budget* for your review. This can help you to understand the nature of the services anticipated, the time that may be spent, and the overall cost. It can also be helpful for budgeting and planning for additional retainers. Knowing the anticipated costs of litigation can help you to make meaningful decisions about which issues to litigate and which to consider resolving through settlement negotiations.

4.20   What is a *trial retainer* and will I have to pay one?

A *trial retainer* is a sum of money paid on your account when it appears your case may not settle and will likely proceed to trial. This retainer is in addition to the initial retainer paid to your attorney. The purpose of the trial retainer is to fund the work needed to prepare for and try the case. Trials are usually expensive and knowing the cost in advance helps you evaluate settlement options

4.21   How do I know whether I should spend the money my lawyer says it will require to go to trial?

One's decision to settle or go to trial is always difficult. Because of the costs of a trial (both economic and emotional), don't make this decision lightly. When considering your options, balance the expense of trial against the likely outcome. Make decisions in a businesslike manner and be careful not to spend a "dime" in legal fees to get a "nickel" from a trial. Be pragmatic. Because of the cost and uncertainty of litigation, a bad settlement is often better than a good verdict.

4.22   If my mother pays my legal fees, will my lawyer give her private information about my divorce?

If someone other than you is paying your legal bills, it is important to inform your lawyer and the person paying that you expect to maintain confidentiality with your attorney. Without your permission, your attorney may not disclose information to others about your case. You are still the client regardless of who pays the bill, and the lawyer should answer only to you.

If you do want your lawyer to communicate with your family members, advise your lawyer and the family members. If you permit the lawyer to discuss the case with family members or others, expect to be charged by your lawyer for the time spent on these calls or meetings.

4.23 Can I ask the court to order my spouse to pay my attorney fees?

Yes, Illinois law allows the court to order your spouse to pay all or a portion of your fees. If one party has resources to pay a lawyer and the other spouse has no money, the spouse with no money can ask for fees from the party with the resources, to place them both on a "level playing field." This allows both parties to adequately defend themselves during the litigation. The court can also award fees as part of the final judgment.

If your case is likely to require costly experts and your spouse has a much greater ability to pay these expenses than you, talk to your lawyer about filing a motion with the court asking your spouse to pay toward these costs while the case is pending. Generally speaking, courts consider both parties' fees and expert costs to be debts of the marriage, to be allocated both during and at the conclusion of the divorce.

4.24 What happens if I don't pay my attorney the fees I promised to pay?

The ethical rules for lawyers allow your attorney to withdraw from representation if you do not comply with your fee agreement. Consequently, it is important that you keep the promises you have made about your account.

If you are having difficulty paying your attorney fees, talk with your attorney about payment options. Consider borrowing the funds, using your credit card, or asking for help from friends and family.

Above all, do not avoid communication with your attorney if you can't make your payment. Avoiding the issue won't help and may seriously disrupt the professional relationship. Be upfront and look for a mutually agreeable solution. Ultimately, if you don't pay your fees, the lawyer can file a petition within the divorce seeking a judgment against you for the fees due. Alternatively, the lawyer can sue you to collect the fees.

4.25 Is there any way I can reduce some of the expenses of getting a divorce?

All litigation is expensive, and divorces are no exception. But there are many methods that can help you control the expense. Here are some suggestions:

Put it in writing. Provide nonurgent information to your attorney by mail, fax, or e-mail. This creates a prompt and accurate record for your file and avoids a phone call and the need for the lawyer to memorialize the discussion by preparing a memo to the file.

Keep your attorney informed. Just as your attorney should keep you up to date on the status of your case, you need to do the same. Keep your lawyer advised about any major developments in your life such as plans to move, moving a boyfriend or girlfriend into your home, change in your employment status, or buying or selling property. During a divorce, your address, phone number, or e-mail address may change. Be sure to update your attorney.

Obtain copies of documents. An important part of litigation includes reviewing documents such as tax returns, account statements, report cards, or medical records. Your attorney will ordinarily be able to request or subpoena these items, but many may be readily available to you directly upon request. Proactively gathering information saves time and thus money.

Consult your attorney's website. If your lawyer has a website, it may be a great source of useful information. The answers to commonly asked questions about the divorce may be found there.

Utilize support professionals. Your lawyer's receptionist, paralegal, legal secretary, or law clerk may be the best person to answer your questions. Although only the attorneys can give you legal advice, other professionals in the office can provide answers to many questions regarding the status of your case or other routine inquiries. Like the communications with your attorney, all communication with any professionals in the firm is strictly confidential.

Consider working with an associate attorney. Although the senior attorneys or partners in a law firm may have more experience, working with an associate attorney may be a good option. Hourly rates for an associate attorney are usually lower than those charged by a senior partner. Frequently, the associate attorney trained under a senior lawyer, developing excellent skills as well as thorough knowledge of the law. Also, senior lawyers typically supervise associates and oversee the case as it progresses. Discuss with the firm the benefits of working with an associate attorney in light of the nature of your case, the expertise of the respective attorneys, and the potential cost savings to you.

Leave a detailed message. If you have an uncomplicated question, leave a message with one of the support staff. The attorney can then answer the question either by calling back, asking a staff member to call back, or e-mailing you. Streamlining communication will usually save money.

Discuss more than one matter during a call. It is not unusual for clients to have many questions during litigation. If your question is not urgent, consider waiting to call until you have more than one question. One call with five questions costs less than five calls with one question each. And although calling your lawyer is expensive, in the long run it is cheaper than avoiding your lawyer to save costs. Without regular communication both ways, problems ensue, causing increased costs and aggravation for both you and your attorney.

Do your homework. Provide information requested by your lawyer in a timely manner. This avoids the cost of follow-up action by your lawyer and the additional expense of extending the time in litigation.

Take a businesslike approach to the case. Weigh your options in a businesslike way. Always do cost-benefit analysis and involve your lawyer in that process. Avoid going to court for long shots (they rarely happen). Your resources (ability to pay fees) are not unlimited and you must use them in the most efficient way possible.

Carefully review your monthly statements. Read your monthly billing statements. If you believe an error has been made, contact your lawyer's office right away to discuss your concerns.

Remain open to settlement. Don't lose sight of the economics of litigation. You never want to spend more in legal fees than the issue warrants. Recognize when your disagreement is about smaller sums of money that will cost more in legal fees than the value of what is disputed. And don't go to court "over the principle of the matter." Principles are very expensive luxuries in litigation and the end result typically leaves you unsatisfied and often poorer for the effort.

5

The Discovery Process

Discovery is one of the least talked about steps in divorce, but it is often the most important. The discovery process allows you and your spouse to meet on a more level playing field, permitting educated decisions concerning settlement or the necessity of trial.

You and your spouse both need accurate information if you hope to reach agreement on any of the issues in your divorce. Similarly, the judge must know all of the facts to make a fair decision. The goal of the discovery process is to accumulate the necessary information to evaluate your case. With this information, you can either negotiate a fair agreement or have all of the facts and documents to argue your case in court.

The discovery process may seem tedious at times because of the need to gather reams of detailed information. Completing it, however, gives the case tremendous clarity. Attorneys and judges simply cannot evaluate a case without the necessary information gathered during discovery.

5.1 What is *discovery*?

As the term suggests, *discovery* is the procedure used to discover the facts of the case. Both lawyers will request information and documents from you, your spouse, potential witnesses, and other persons. Each case is different, and depending upon the issues or circumstances, lawyers use different discovery methods.

Formal discovery must be distinguished from *informal investigation.* Formal discovery is governed by the rules of the Illinois Supreme Court. The Supreme Court dictates all of the guidelines and rules that apply to gathering information prior to trial. In contrast, lawyers also informally investigate the facts of their case. They might do this by interviewing witnesses, doing Internet research, hiring a private investigator, or accumulating facts through other databases available to the public.

5.2   What types of discovery might be done by my lawyer or my spouse's lawyer?

Types of discovery include:

Interrogatories. Interrogatories are written questions that must be answered by a party, under oath, within twenty-eight days of the request. Interrogatories might ask for routine financial information such as any bank accounts that you have, or information concerning anything else that is relevant to the case.

Request for production of documents. This discovery procedure requires a party to produce copies of documents that are in their possession or control. The requested party must comply within twenty-eight days. If a party has good cause, reasonable extensions are granted.

Requests for admissions of fact or genuineness of documents. This procedure requires a party to admit or deny certain facts within twenty-eight days of the request for the admission. If the request isn't answered within twenty-eight days, the fact is deemed admitted. Also, the rules require a party to admit the genuineness or authenticity of documents presented.

Subpoena of documents. The rules allow either party to issue a subpoena to a third party, which requires the third party to produce copies of requested records or appear for a deposition and answer questions in person.

Depositions. Depositions are informal court proceedings that are conducted outside the presence of the judge, which allow the attorneys to ask questions of the other party or a third person who has been subpoenaed. Lawyers usually conduct depositions at their office. A court reporter is present at the deposition and records all answers, which can be typed out in a transcript of the testimony if requested.

At the beginning of the deposition, the witness is sworn in by the court reporter, and all answers are given under oath, just like in a court proceeding. Although the judge ordinarily does not review the deposition transcript, the sworn testimony can be used to discredit the witness if they change their answer at trial. By court rules in Illinois, depositions cannot last more than three hours without prior permission by the judge. Frequently, they are much shorter than the three-hour time limit.

5.3 My lawyer says we need to start by completing a *financial affidavit*. What is this document and how is it used?

A *financial affidavit* is a statewide form created by our Supreme Court to summarize a party's income, expenses, debts, and property. The affidavit must be answered truthfully to the best of the party's knowledge. It is a snapshot or overview of the basic financial circumstances of the party completing the form. Additionally, supporting documents are to be attached to the form. Both parties need to complete and exchange the affidavit at the beginning of the case. By doing so, it helps the lawyers better focus their analysis and investigation. The early exchange of the financial affidavit allows the lawyers to start developing settlement strategies immediately.

5.4 I cannot complete the financial affidavit because all of the information is in the possession of my spouse. What do I do?

It's not uncommon for one spouse to keep the other spouse in the dark regarding family finances. If that is the case, do your best to answer the questions you do know, and note on the form which information is in the possession of your spouse. The court will not penalize you for your lack of knowledge. Make sure to advise your lawyer if you are denied access to family financial information.

5.5 I have reviewed my spouse's financial affidavit and see many untrue statements. What are the consequences for my spouse's false information?

The rules provide that "If a party intentionally or recklessly files an inaccurate or misleading financial affidavit, the court shall impose significant penalties and sanctions including, but not limited to, cost and attorney's fees." Besides exposing themselves to sanctions, parties who make misrepresentations hurt their credibility with the judge and may be punished by harsh rulings that reflect the judge's mistrust. Make sure to advise your lawyer of the false statements and provide any proof or information to corroborate the falseness of your spouse's misrepresentations.

5.6   I am worried that our personal financial information will be filed in the court file and subject me to identity theft. How do I protect my financial privacy?

Neither your financial affidavit, its attachments, nor any other discovery information will be filed in the court file. It is exchanged between the lawyers and kept private in the lawyers' file. Sometimes people have concerns about sensitive business information being exchanged. In that event, the concerned party will often seek a court order known as a *protective order* protecting the privacy of the information and directing all parties not to disclose the information without court permission.

5.7   What factors does my lawyer consider in choosing a particular type of discovery option?

Lawyers consider a number of different factors when developing a discovery action plan. Here are some factors they might consider in choosing a particular method of discovery:

The types of issues in dispute. For example, discovery related to parenting issues would likely be more intensive than discovery in a dispute over the division of personal property.

How much access you and your spouse have to needed information. If all of the necessary information is available to both parties, in-depth discovery is unnecessary. On the other hand, if one of the parties has no information about the family finances, that party will need to undertake more-exhaustive discovery process.

The level of cooperation in sharing information. Where one of the parties has information and fails to voluntarily share the information, formal discovery is a way to force the disclosure. Voluntary and cooperative disclosures may avoid the necessity of doing any discovery.

The nature of the conflict. High-conflict cases that are headed for trial require more discovery. For example, a case that is likely to settle might not require a deposition because the necessary information can be obtained by reviewing records. But in a case going to trial, depositions are helpful (depending upon the issues at stake).

The budget available for performing discovery. Some types of discovery cost more than other types. A subpoena, for example, is less expensive than a deposition, which can cost thousands of dollars, considering the preparation time, attendance at the deposition, and court reporter services.

Discuss with your lawyer his or her thoughts on the most efficient discovery method available for your case.

5.8 How long does the discovery process take?

Discovery can take anywhere from a few weeks to many months, depending upon the complexity of the case, the cooperation of you and your spouse, and whether expert witnesses are involved. Ideally, discovery should commence as soon as the attorney can identify the disputed issues and the nature of the conflict.

5.9 My lawyer insists that we conduct discovery, but I don't want to spend the time and money on it. Is it really necessary?

The discovery process can be critical to a successful outcome in your case for several reasons:

- It increases the likelihood that any agreements reached are based on accurate information.

- It provides necessary information for deciding whether to settle or proceed to trial.

- It avoids surprises at trial, such as unexpected witness testimony.

Discovery, although potentially expensive, is often critical. Discuss ways to make the process more efficient. Ask your attorney what he or she is trying to achieve by undertaking a particular discovery plan. Perhaps you can informally gather the necessary information. You should be a partner in the litigation, not just a bystander. Your input is helpful.

5.10 I just received interrogatories and requests that I produce documents. My lawyer wants me to respond within two weeks. I am terrible with paperwork. What can I do?

Answering your discovery promptly will help speed up your case and control your legal fees. There are steps you can take to make this task easier. The process may seem overwhelming, but if you break the project into smaller tasks, it makes the job easier.

First, look at all of the questions. Many of them will not apply or your answers will be a simple "yes" or "no." Exclude all of the questions that don't apply. Often, lawyers use boiler-plate forms that ask for information about items you don't own. These questions can be immediately excluded.

Seek help while you are going through your divorce. Ask a friend to help. Or hire a professional divorce coach. Chances are that you will make great progress in just a couple of hours with a friend or assistant helping you. Ask your lawyer whether a paralegal in the office can help you organize the needed information or determine whether some of it can be provided at a later date.

The rules grant twenty-eight days to respond to discovery requests. If you will not be able to comply on time, you may be entitled to reasonable extensions. But extensions should be the exception and not the rule. Procrastination is not a legitimate reason to delay compliance. Delays often lead to frustration by clients and lawyers and irritate judges as well. Do your best to provide the information in a timely manner, with the help of others if necessary.

5.11 My spouse's lawyer intends to subpoena my medical records. Aren't these private?

Illinois protects the privacy of your medical and psychological records; these records are not automatically available to your spouse. If the records are sought to harass you or to satisfy your spouse's curiosity, the judge will likely deny their disclosure. In order for your spouse to access your records, the records must be relevant to one of the issues in the case. If you are requesting maintenance or if your health is an issue, these records may be relevant. Or, if parenting issues are contested, information about your health may be important.

Talk with your lawyer about your rights. Procedures exist to block a subpoena seeking medical information. Sometimes the court will limit the disclosure entirely. Other times, the judge will agree to review the records first to determine if your right to privacy outweighs the importance of the information.

5.12 It's been two months since my lawyer sent interrogatories to my spouse, and we still don't have my spouse's answers. I answered mine on time. Is there anything that can be done to speed up the process?

Your spouse's failure to follow the rules of discovery can add to both the frustration and expense of the divorce. If your spouse procrastinates or plays games, you may need to enforce compliance by court order. Talk with your attorney about filing a *motion to compel,* a court order forcing your spouse to comply. Attorney fees caused by your spouse's tardy response may be awarded.

Ask your lawyer whether a subpoena to your spouse's employer or a financial institution would be a more efficient way to get necessary information. Sometimes it is easier and more cost effective to get the desired information from third parties.

5.13 I have some information on my Facebook page that is embarrassing and will hurt my case. Is it okay if I delete my incriminating posts?

You may not destroy information that could be used as evidence by either you or your spouse. This is known as *spoliation of evidence* and will subject you to harsh penalties. Make sure to be cautious about your use of social media both before and during the divorce. Remember: anything you post can be used against you if it is relevant to the case. Similarly, be very careful responding to your spouse via text message. Understand that any angry response to your spouse's taunts will likely be shared with the court.

5.14　My lawyer just notified me the other attorney wants to take my deposition. What can I expect?

A deposition allows an attorney to personally ask you questions that you must answer under oath. The deposition is conducted outside of court, and a court reporter is present to record your testimony. Both attorneys will appear and your spouse has a right to be present as well.

Your spouse's attorney may ask you questions about anything that is relevant or could lead to relevant information. Although the scope of the questioning is broad, it doesn't mean that the opposing attorney can harass you with embarrassing questions. Your attorney will be present and will object to improper questions. Speak with your attorney about how you should prepare and what you can expect.

Your attorney may ask you questions after your spouse's attorney finishes questioning you, or he or she may choose not to ask you questions. It is generally uncommon for your attorney to ask you questions (he or she can get information privately without placing your answers on the record). Sometimes your attorney may ask questions to clarify your testimony if you mistakenly said something that might be later taken out of context.

At the conclusion of the deposition, you will be asked whether you want to review and sign the transcript or whether you waive your right to do so. If you choose to review the transcript, you can correct typographical errors but you cannot change your testimony. Many lawyers advise their clients to waive the right to review and sign the transcript.

5.15　What is the purpose of a deposition?

A deposition serves several important purposes:

To gather information. A deposition allows the opposing attorney to gather information directly from the mouth of the witness. This information helps the attorney prepare the case for trial.

To avoid surprises at trial. The deposition captures the witness's sworn testimony before trial. If the witness later changes his or her testimony at trial, your spouse's lawyer can ask the witness about the earlier inconsistency. The process of challenging a witness's credibility based on a prior inconsistent statement is known as *impeaching the witness.*

To evaluate the witness. The deposition allows an attorney to assess the demeanor of the witness. For example, if your spouse is a likeable witness, your attorney may recommend avoiding trial if an adequate settlement proposal is presented. Conversely, if your spouse is evasive and argumentative, your attorney may be more confident going to trial.

To preserve testimony. The rules allow the use of a deposition in the event a witness later becomes unavailable.

Depositions can be essential tools in a contested divorce case, especially when a case is likely to proceed to trial.

5.16 Will my deposition testimony be used against me when we go to court?

If you are called as a witness at your trial and you testify differently from your deposition testimony, the opposing attorney can use your deposition testimony to challenge your credibility: "Are you lying now or were you lying then?" It is important to review your deposition prior to testifying at trial to make sure your testimony remains consistent. A review of the transcript will also give you some idea of the questions that may be asked at trial.

5.17 Will the judge read the depositions?

Unless a witness becomes unavailable for trial or gives conflicting testimony at trial, it is unlikely that the judge will ever read the depositions.

5.18 How should I prepare for my deposition?

To prepare, review the important documents in your case, such as any pleadings, your answers to interrogatories, and your financial affidavit. Gather and review any documents you've been asked to provide at your deposition. Deliver them to your attorney in advance of your deposition for copying and review.

Also, schedule an appointment with your attorney to discuss the format of the deposition. Discuss the protocol for the deposition and what topics or questions the attorney generally anticipates. If you are troubled by certain topics or potential questions, discuss these with your attorney at this meeting.

At the deposition, you must answer the questions, even if they might be embarrassing or uncomfortable. If your attorney objects to a question during the deposition, stop talking and wait for instructions. Your attorney may direct you not to answer the question.

If you don't know the answer to a question it is appropriate to say so. If you don't remember something, don't guess, just indicate that you don't remember. But if you know an answer, you must answer unless the question requires you to admit an illegal activity. If there are any issues involving illegal conduct, devise a strategy with your attorney in advance of the deposition. For example, the attorney might instruct you to exercise your constitutional right to remain silent. Find out about the consequences of not answering versus admitting to the illegal conduct.

5.19   What will I be asked?

The questions will depend on the issues. If parenting time and decision-making responsibility is an issue, you will be asked questions about past parenting practices or incidents relating to the children. If financial issues are at the heart of the case, you will be asked questions about your income or property. Often, questions will be mundane, for example, questions about budgetary matters. Other times, the questions will be more lurid, for example, questions about money spent on extramarital relationships. Meet with your attorney before the deposition to get an idea of the topics that your attorney expects the opposing attorney will cover.

5.20   What if I give incorrect information in my deposition?

You will be under oath during your deposition, so make sure that you answer all questions truthfully. If you give incorrect information by mistake, contact your attorney as soon as you realize the error. If you lie during your deposition, it is considered perjury and is illegal. Criminal consequences aside, getting caught in a lie will cause you to lose credibility with the judge, rendering your testimony worthless. Don't risk it.

5.21 What else do I need to know about having my deposition taken?

The following suggestions will help you to give a successful deposition:

- Prepare for your deposition by reviewing and providing necessary documents and prepping for the deposition with your lawyer.

- Get a good night's sleep the night before. Eat a healthly meal to sustain your energy, as the deposition may be exhausting.

- Arrive early for your deposition so that you have time to get comfortable with your surroundings.

- Relax. You are going to be asked questions about matters you're familiar with. Your deposition is likely to begin with routine matters such as your education and work history.

- Tell the truth.

- Stay calm. Your spouse's lawyer will be judging your credibility and demeanor.

- Don't argue with the attorneys or let them get under your skin. Maintain good self-control. Act unconcerned even if you think things are not going well.

- Don't be defensive or overanalyze the purpose of the questions: "I wonder what he's getting at here?" Just answer the questions to the best of your ability.

- Listen carefully to the entire question. Do not try to anticipate questions or start thinking about your answer before the attorney has finished asking the question.

- Take your time and carefully consider the question before answering. There is no need to hurry.

- If you don't understand the question, ask that it be repeated or rephrased.

- Answer the question directly. If the question calls only for "yes" or "no," answer yes or no. Don't ramble beyond the question being asked.

- Don't volunteer information. If the opposing lawyer wants to elicit more information, he or she will ask follow-up questions.

- If you do not know or cannot remember the answer, say so. That is an adequate answer.

- Do not guess, and if you give an "educated guess" about something, indicate that it is just that.

- If your answer is an estimate or approximation, say so.

- Do not let the opposing attorney pin you down to anything you are not sure about. For example, if you cannot remember the number of times an event occurred, say that. If the attorney asks you if it happened more than ten times, answer only if you can. If you can provide a range (more than ten but less than twenty) with reasonable certainty, you may do so.

- If an attorney mischaracterizes something you said earlier, say so. "I didn't say that, I said…"

- Speak clearly and loudly enough for everyone to hear you.

- Answer all questions with words, rather than gestures or sounds. "Uh-huh" is difficult for the court reporter to distinguish from "unh-unh" and may result in inaccuracies in the transcript.

- If you need a break at any point in the deposition, you have the right to request one. You can talk to your attorney during such a break.

- Remember that the purpose of your deposition is to support a good outcome in your case. Completing it will help your case to move forward.

5.22 Are depositions always necessary? Does every witness have to be deposed?

Depositions are usually unnecessary if you and your spouse agree on most of the facts and are moving toward a settlement. They are also less necessary in cases with uncomplicated issues. Depositions are more vital in cases where parenting issues are disputed or where there are complex financial issues.

5.23   Will I get a copy of the depositions in my case?

You can request that the court reporter type the transcript. If you want a copy of the transcript, ask your attorney to order one. The price of the transcript can cost several hundred dollars, so have the attorney determine an estimated cost in advance. If your case proceeds to trial, you will need to order the transcript to review your testimony prior to trial.

6

Mediation and Negotiation

Some couples need a judge to decide their case, but many others can work things out on their own. Going to trial and having a judge make decisions is not inevitable. In fact, most Illinois divorce cases settle without the need for a trial. *Mediation* and *negotiation* allow you and your spouse to resolve your disputed issues and reach a settlement/agreement without the need for a judge to decide the case. This has many advantages. A settlement allows you to achieve a mutually satisfying agreement, a known outcome with little risk of appeal, and usually lowers your legal fees. Despite the circumstances that led to the end of your marriage, it might be possible for your divorce to conclude peacefully with the help of these tools.

6.1 What is the difference between *mediation* and *negotiation*?

Both mediation and negotiation help you resolve your divorce by agreement rather than going to trial. *Mediation* uses a mediator—a neutral third party—who helps you and your spouse resolve your issues directly. The mediation process involves conferences between you, your spouse, and the mediator. With the mediator's help, you and your spouse discuss all of the issues and determine if there are any disputes. If there are, the mediator helps you try to resolve them amicably. Lawyers rarely attend mediation sessions in Illinois. *Negotiating,* in contrast, actively involves attorneys, who draft proposals or set up meetings to negotiate the contested issues.

And of course, you and your spouse can work things out on your own, without the need of a mediator or lawyers. Try sitting down at the kitchen table and see how far you both can get on your own before involving these third parties. However, if there are any issues of domestic violence or other control issues, it is recommended that you go straight to your lawyer for help.

6.2 How are mediation and negotiation different from a collaborative divorce?

Collaborative law is a method of resolving a divorce case without going to court. You and your spouse each hire your own attorney, who is trained in the collaborative law process. Both you and your spouse agree to negotiate, and agree that in the event either of you decides to take the case to court, both of you must fire your collaborative lawyers and start over with new lawyers. This system is designed to act as a deterrent against either of you giving up on the negotiations; it is inconvenient and expensive to start over with new lawyers.

Often, people in the collaborative process enlist the support of other professionals, such as an independent financial advisor or coaches, to help throughout the process. Although the collaborative process may be lengthy, its goal is to help the parties refocus from conflict toward finding solutions. The attorneys become a part of the team supporting settlement rather than act as advocates.

Collaborative law is controversial in some segments of the legal community. Some lawyers believe it is an inherent conflict of interest to require the lawyer to either "bless" a settlement proposal or withdraw from the case. Many lawyers are troubled by the requirement that a client start over with a new lawyer if they think they need help from a judge. The collaborative process may also pose problems when one of the parties is not honest or forthcoming with accurate financial information. Illinois has yet to popularly embrace collaborative divorce. If you are interested in this process, find an attorney who has knowledge about the process and discuss the pros and cons.

6.3   What does mediation involve? What will I have to do and how long will it take?

The mediator will explain the process at the start of the first mediation session. The mediator will outline the ground rules designed to ensure you will be treated respectfully and given an opportunity to be heard. Although mediation was traditionally used to resolve parenting issues, today many use mediation to resolve financial issues as well.

The length of the process depends upon many of the same factors that affect the length of your divorce. These include the number of disputed issues, the complexity of these issues, and the willingness of each of you to work toward an agreement. The process may require you both to do homework: prepare budgets, provide income information, and provide any other information to help the mediator help you settle the case.

Your case could settle after just a couple of mediation sessions or it might require a series of meetings. It is common for the mediator to clarify at the close of each session whether both parties are willing to continue with another session.

6.4   Does mediation and negotiation shorten my divorce process?

When a judge decides the issues in your divorce, there are many opportunities for delay. The court system is usually overburdened with people needing help from the judge. A negotiated or mediated agreement avoids the following problems inherent with a trial:

- Waiting for the trial date, which sometimes may be many months away

- Losing a previously scheduled trial date if another matter, considered more urgent, comes before the court on your scheduled trial date

- Having to return to court on a later, second date if your trial is not completed on the day it is scheduled

- Waiting for the judge's ruling on your case

- Needing additional court hearings after your trial to resolve disputes about the intention of your judge's rulings, issues that were overlooked, or disagreement regarding the language of the decree

Each one of these events holds the possibility of delaying your divorce by days, weeks, or even months. Mediating or negotiating the terms of your divorce decree can eliminate these delays.

6.5 How can mediation and negotiation lower the costs of my divorce?

In a nutshell, the less time your attorney spends on your case, the lower the legal fees. If your case is not settled by agreement, you will be going to trial. If there are many issues in your case or if they are complex, the attorney fees and other costs of going to trial can be tremendous.

By settling your case without going to trial, you may be able to save thousands of dollars in legal fees. Ask your attorney for a litigation budget that sets forth the potential costs of going to trial, so that you have some idea of these costs when deciding whether to settle an issue or to take it to trial before a judge.

6.6 Are there other benefits to mediating or negotiating a settlement?

Yes. A divorce resolved by a mediated or negotiated agreement can have these additional benefits:

Recognizing common goals. Mediation and negotiation allow for brainstorming between the parties and lawyers. Looking at all possible solutions, even the impractical ones, invites creative solutions to common goals. For example, suppose you and your spouse both agree that you need to pay your spouse some amount of equity for the family home you will keep, but you have no cash to make the payment. Together, you might come up with a number of options for accomplishing your goal and select the best one. Contrast this with the judge who simply orders you to pay the money without considering all of the possible options.

Addressing the unique circumstances of your situation. Rather than using a one-size-fits-all approach as a judge might do, a settlement reached by agreement allows you and your spouse to consider the unique circumstances of your situation in formulating a good outcome. For example, regarding who has the child for the Thanksgiving holiday, the judge will likely order you to alternate the holiday each year, even though you both would have preferred to have your child share the day.

Creating a safe place for communication. Mediation and negotiation give each party an opportunity to be heard. Perhaps you and your spouse have not yet had an opportunity to share directly your concerns about settlement. For example, you might be worried about how the temporary parenting time arrangement is impacting your children, but have not yet talked to your spouse about it. A mediation session or settlement conference can be a safe place for you and your spouse to communicate your concerns about your children or your finances.

Fulfilling your children's needs. You may see that your children would be better served if you and your spouse decide their future rather than have it decided by a judge who does not know, love, and understand your children like the two of you do. Judges do their best to be fair, but without knowing the temperaments and personalities of your children, it is hard for them to structure a parenting plan that maximizes the children's interest.

Eliminating the risk and uncertainty of trial. If a judge decides the outcome of your divorce, you give up control over the terms of the settlement. The decisions are left in the hands of the judge. And, despite their best efforts, judges sometimes make mistakes. If you and your spouse reach agreement, however, you have the power to eliminate the risk of an uncertain outcome.

Reducing the risk of harm to your children. If your case goes to trial, it is likely that you and your spouse will give testimony that will be upsetting to each other. As the conflict increases, the relationship between you and your spouse inevitably deteriorates. This can be harmful to your children. Contrast this with mediation or settlement negotiations, in which you open your communication and seek to reach agreement. It is not unusual for the relationship between the parents to improve as the professionals create a safe environment for rebuilding communication and reaching agreements in the best interest of a child.

Having the support of professionals. Using trained professionals, such as mediators and lawyers, to support you can help you reach a settlement that you might think is impossible. These professionals have skills to help you focus on what is most important to you, and shift your attention away from irrelevant facts. They understand the law and know the possible outcomes if your case goes to trial.

Lowering stress. The process of preparing for and going to court is inherently stressful. Add to this the mounting costs and the uncertainly of the result. Although negotiation or mediation is not stress free, it usually pales in comparison.

Achieving closure. When you are going through a divorce, the process can feel as though it is taking an eternity. By reaching agreement, you and your spouse are better able to put the divorce behind you and move forward with your lives.

6.7   Is mediation mandatory?

Relatively early in the case, the judge will inquire whether custody or parenting issues have been resolved. If not, the judge will require the two of you to attend mediation on the unresolved parental responsibility issues. The Illinois Supreme Court Rules require mediation before presenting those issues to the judge. Mediation, which is advisable in many instances, is not mandatory for financial disputes.

6.8   What if I want to try mediation and my spouse doesn't?

Unless mediation is court ordered to resolve a parenting issue, your spouse is not required to participate. You may want to remind your spouse of the benefits and the cost savings. However, if he or she is reluctant, it will be a waste of time to further pursue the issue and you should focus on using your lawyer to negotiate an agreement.

6.9   Both my spouse and I want to mediate our financial issues, but my lawyer says it is a bad idea. How can mediation be a bad idea?

Although mediation is often beneficial, it isn't always a good idea. If, for example, there are concerns about hidden assets or income, or other issues that require in-depth investigation, mediation may expose you to risk. Also, if you are very conciliatory, your lawyer may worry that you might be taken advantage of. In that instance, negotiation may be more preferable, allowing more involvement by the attorney.

6.10 My lawyer wants to get trial dates but I want to negotiate. Why does my attorney insist on going to court?

First, ask your attorney his or her reasoning. It may be tactical. For example, perhaps your attorney knows that your spouse's attorney perpetually delays cases and is frequently unprepared. By getting an earlier trial date, it may force the procrastinating attorney to conclude the case sooner. Or perhaps your attorney believes that your spouse is very manipulative and that he or she will not likely negotiate in good faith. By setting a trial date, it still allows you the ability to negotiate in the meantime, but provides a backstop in the event your attorney's concerns are validated.

Other times, however, negotiation is a sensible option and some attorneys are just quarrelsome, preferring to fight rather than negotiate. Unless your lawyer's reasons for not negotiating are sound, consider getting a different lawyer who will support your desire to work things out.

6.11 My spouse abused me and I am afraid to participate in mediation. Should I participate anyway?

If you have been a victim of domestic violence, mediation may be inappropriate. In the event you are worried about your safety, talk to your lawyer about avoiding mediation.

Prior to allowing mediation to proceed, any mediator should determine whether you have been a victim of domestic violence. This is critical for the mediator to both assess your safety and ensure that the balance of power in the mediation process is maintained.

If you feel threatened or intimidated by your spouse but still want to proceed with mediation, talk to your lawyer about the possibility of him or her attending the mediation sessions with you. Request to have the mediation occur at your lawyer's office, where you feel more comfortable. Also ask about mediating with your spouse being in a separate room.

If you do participate in mediation, insist that your mediator have a good understanding of the dynamics of domestic abuse and how they can impact the mediation process.

6.12 What training and credentials do mediators have?

There is no license requirement for a mediator to practice in Illinois. The background of mediators varies. Some are lawyers; many come from other backgrounds such as counseling. Some counties certify mediators based upon certain qualifications. Ask your attorney for help in finding a qualified mediator who has completed training in mediating family law cases. The availability of mediators also varies depending upon where you live.

6.13 What types of issues can be mediated or negotiated?

All of the issues in your case can be mediated or negotiated. However, in advance of any mediation or negotiation session, you should discuss with your lawyer which issues will be mediated or negotiated.

Also, if you mediate, don't feel pressured to agree: reserve the right to consult with your attorney prior to making any final decisions. Even if you think the proposal may be satisfactory, there may be certain implications that you didn't think about when the proposal was presented to you.

Talk with your lawyer in advance of any mediation about parenting issues to be absolutely clear about the impact of those decisions on child support. Agreeing to certain parenting arrangements can affect child support, and you should not negotiate on parental decision making and parenting time without fully discussing the consequences in advance of the mediation sessions.

6.14 What is the role of my attorney in the mediation process?

The role of your attorney in the mediation process will vary depending upon your situation. Your attorney can assist you by identifying appropriate issues for mediation and those issues that are better left to negotiation or to the judge. The attorney should prepare you prior to your first mediation session and discuss the parameters of the process. The attorney also should be available to consult with you during the process. After a session, call your attorney and discuss your progress and possible settlement scenarios. In all cases it is important that your attorney review any agreements discussed in mediation before a final agreement is reached.

6.15　How do I prepare for mediation?

As mentioned earlier, the most important way to prepare is to meet with your attorney in advance of the first session to identify the issues and possible settlement scenarios. Make a list of the issues important to you. The best way to move closer to settlement is:

- Be forward-looking.
- Think ahead to your desired outcome.
- Approach mediation with an open mind.

6.16　Do our children attend the mediation sessions?

In most cases your children will not participate in the mediation. However, your case might be an exception if you have an older child who is sufficiently mature to participate in the process. If you think your child should be involved, talk to your lawyer and your mediator about the potential risks and benefits of including him or her in the process.

6.17　I want my attorney to look over the agreements my spouse and I discussed in mediation before I give my final approval. Is this possible?

Yes. It is critical that your attorney review the agreement prior to your giving final consent. The review is necessary to ensure that you understand the terms of the settlement and its implications, and that the agreement complies with Illinois law.

6.18　Who pays for mediation?

You or your spouse pays the mediator. Often it is a shared expense. Expect your mediator to address the matter of fees before or at your first session.

6.19   What if mediation fails?

If mediation is unsuccessful, you still may be able to settle your case through negotiations between the attorneys. Also, you and your spouse can agree to preserve the settlements that were reached and to take only the remaining disputed issues to the judge for trial.

6.20   What is *arbitration*?

Like mediation, *arbitration* is an alternative dispute resource. With arbitration, disputed issues are presented to either an individual arbitrator or a panel of arbitrators who will decide the contested issues as "private judges." Facts are presented and the lawyers argue the case. Usually, arbitration is more informal than a formal hearing before a judge, and the rules of evidence are relaxed. The parties agree to be bound by the arbitrator's ruling or agree that if one of them rejects the ruling, some sanction will apply, such as the payment of the prevailing party's fees if the loser then proceeds to court. Both parties must agree to arbitration. It is a creative method to resolve contested issues more quickly than if they are presented to a judge a formal hearing.

6.21   What is a *settlement conference*?

A *settlement conference,* also known as a *four-way conference,* is a meeting between you, your spouse, and your lawyers. The meeting is designed to help resolve the issues of your divorce. In some cases, a professional, such as an accountant, may participate.

Settlement conferences are most effective when both parties and their attorneys see the potential for a negotiated resolution and have the necessary information to accomplish that goal. Often, these conferences are valuable early in the case to identify the contested issues and develop a framework for methods of resolution.

For example, if the parties and lawyers can determine at an early meeting that allocation of parenting time is not an issue, one of the lawyers can start preparing a draft parenting plan. Or the parties can determine that parenting time issues exist and agree to immediately start the mediation process rather than wait for the court to order it a few months down the road. Perhaps there is a family business. The lawyers can agree on a joint mutual business evaluator to value the business and come up with a game plan to value the other assets. This cooperative approach to the divorce saves time and money.

6.22 Why should I consider a settlement conference when the attorneys can negotiate through letters and phone calls?

A settlement conference eliminates the delays that occur when negotiation takes place through correspondence and calls between the attorneys. Rather than waiting days or weeks for a response, you can receive a response on a proposal in a matter of minutes.

A settlement conference also enables you to use your own words to explain the reasoning behind your requests. You are also able to provide information immediately to expedite the process.

6.23 How do I prepare for my settlement conference?

Being well prepared for the settlement conference can help you make the most of this opportunity. Consider the following:

- If your attorney has asked you for a current pay stub, tax return, debt amounts, asset values, or other documentation, make sure it is provided prior to the meeting.

- Discuss topics of concern with your attorney in advance. Your lawyer can assist you in understanding your rights under the law so that you can have realistic expectations for the outcome of negotiations.

- Have a positive attitude, a listening ear, and an open mind. Come with the attitude that your case will settle. Listen to your spouse's concerns, and then share your position. Keep your emotions in check. Resist the urge to interrupt.

Few cases settle without each side demonstrating flexibility and a willingness to compromise. Most cases settle when the parties (and their lawyers) bring these qualities to the process.

6.24 What will happen at my settlement conference?

Typically, the conference will be held at the office of one of the attorneys, with both parties and lawyers present. Sometimes the meeting may occur at the courthouse before or after the business of the day is concluded. If there are a number of issues to be discussed, an agenda may be used to keep the focus on relevant topics. From time to time throughout the conference, you and your attorney may meet alone to consult as needed. If additional information is needed to reach agreement, some issues may be set aside for later discussion.

The length of the conference depends upon the number of issues to be resolved, the complexity of the issues, and the willingness of the parties and lawyers to communicate effectively. An effort is made to confirm which issues are resolved and which issues remain disputed. Then, one by one, the issues are addressed.

6.25 What is the role of my attorney in the settlement conference?

Your attorney is your advocate during the settlement conference. You can count on him or her to support you throughout the process, to see that important issues are addressed, and to counsel you privately outside of the presence of your spouse and his or her lawyer.

6.26 Why is my lawyer appearing so friendly with my spouse and her lawyer?

Successful negotiations rely upon building trust between the parties working toward agreement. Your lawyer may be respectful or pleasant toward your spouse or your spouse's lawyer to promote a good outcome for you. Don't misinterpret your lawyer's friendliness as a betrayal to you. Remember the old adages, "You can catch more flies with honey" and "A smile can often get more done than a threat."

6.27 Does the judge ever assist in negotiations?

When you and your spouse reach an impasse, sometimes it is helpful to solicit the opinion of the judge concerning a resolution. Often known as a *pretrial conference,* this informal meeting allows the lawyers to discuss the contested issues with the judge, soliciting how the judge might rule if the issues were presented at trial. This process allows the parties to gauge the judge's assessment of the issues, which is helpful as part of the negotiations.

Usually these conferences are conducted in the judge's chambers, without either you or your spouse present. You and your spouse are usually excluded from this conference because judges feel that the attorneys will be more likely to discuss the strengths and weaknesses of their position outside of the presence of their respective clients. Trust your attorney to advocate for you.

6.28 What happens if my spouse and I settle some but not all of the issues in our divorce?

Most judges permit you and your spouse to maintain the agreements you have reached and present only those issues you are unable to resolve. This is a pragmatic way of streamlining your case. Get as far as you can on your own, and let the judge dispose of the remaining contested matters.

6.29 If my spouse and I reach an agreement, how long will it take before we can go before the judge to conclude the case?

If a settlement is reached through negotiation or mediation, one of the attorneys will put the agreement in writing for approval by you and your spouse. In most cases, the court will conduct a final prove-up hearing within thirty days after you conclude your agreement.

7

Emergency:
When You Fear Your Spouse

Because volatile emotions can arise when a divorce starts, emergency issues are common. People often panic and behave poorly. Otherwise rational and thoughtful people sometimes act inappropriately. In other instances, toxic characters or personality disorders manifest under the stress and trauma of the breakup. People take money, make threats, and revert to childlike selfish behavior.

When facing an emergency, focus on an appropriate response. Don't panic or get paralyzed by fear; take action to protect yourself. Illinois law provides many remedies that can help.

7.1 I'm afraid my abusive spouse will try to hurt me and/ or our children if I say I want a divorce. What can I do legally to protect my children and myself?

Develop a safety plan for you and your children. In addition to meeting with an attorney at your first opportunity, develop a plan in the event you and your children need to escape your home. A good way to do this is to seek support from an agency that helps victims of domestic violence. Call the Illinois Coalition Against Domestic Violence at (877) 863-6338 or visit their website at (www.ilcadv.org) to get more information about the domestic violence program closest to you.

Find a lawyer who understands domestic violence. Often, your local domestic violence agency can help with a referral to an attorney. Talk to your lawyer about the concerns for your safety and that of your children. Ask your lawyer about an *order for protection*. This is a powerful court order that offers you a number of temporary protections, including: exclusive possession of your home, all parenting time and decision making for your children, and a court order requiring your spouse to physically stay away from you. If your spouse violates this order, you can dial 911 and your spouse will be immediately arrested.

You can seek an order of protection without a lawyer as well. If you feel you may need such an order, contact your local clerk of the court to find out about procedures for obtaining such an order without a lawyer.

7.2   I am afraid to meet with a lawyer because I am terrified my spouse will find out and become violent. What should I do?

Immediately schedule an initial consultation with an attorney experienced in domestic violence situations. When you schedule the appointment, let the firm know your situation and don't leave any contact information that might inadvertently tip off your spouse about the consultation. Also, try to schedule the appointment early in the morning on a weekday in the event the attorney recommends seeking an immediate order of protection. You could proceed from the appointment directly to the courthouse to obtain one.

Let your attorney know your safety concerns immediately. If you take no action because you fear the consequences, nothing will change for you. The laws recognize the danger of domestic violence and provide strong remedies for your protection. Don't continue to live in an abusive relationship; learn your options by consulting with an attorney trained in this area of law.

7.3   I want to give my attorney all necessary information so my children and I are safe. What does this include?

Provide your attorney with complete information about the history, background, nature, and evidence of your abuse, including:

- The types of abuse (for example, physical, sexual, verbal, financial, mental, emotional)

- A narrative of the specifics of all abuse, including: the dates, locations, and what happened
- Whether you were ever treated medically for the abuse
- Any police reports or prior arrest records
- Evidence of the abuse (text messages, e-mails, letters, notes, pictures, or journal entries)
- Any witnesses to the abuse
- Any statements made by your spouse admitting the abuse
- Alcohol or drug abuse
- The presence of guns or other weapons

Your lawyer needs evidence to successfully protect you and your children. The more information you provide, the more likely the court will assist you.

7.4   I'm not ready to hire a lawyer for a divorce, but I am afraid my spouse is going to get violent in the meantime. What can I do?

You don't need to file for divorce to obtain an order of protection. In fact, you don't even need to be married to be eligible for protection. You only need show you have a qualifying relationship with the other party. With an order of protection, a judge may order your spouse out of your home, grant you all parenting time and decision-making rights for your children, and order your spouse to stay away from you. This type of order is called an *emergency order of protection*. Courts throughout the state provide trained court assistants to help you obtain the order. The emergency order of protection will remain in place for twenty-one days. You can obtain more information about this process by calling the clerk of the circuit court where you live.

7.5   What's the difference between an *order of protection* and a *restraining order*?

Orders of protection and *restraining orders* both protect people from their spouse's bad conduct. Although a restraining order or an order of protection can be obtained without notice, your spouse has a right to a later hearing to determine whether the order of protection or restraining order should remain in place.

Enforcement is the biggest difference between these two types of protective orders. If an order of protection is violated, the police will immediately enforce the order by arresting your spouse. In contrast, a restraining order can only be enforced through a court proceeding alleging violation of the order. This type of procedure takes weeks or longer. If you fear for your physical safety, seek an order of protection rather than a restraining order.

Often, during negotiations, attorneys will negotiate a dismissal of the order of protection in exchange for an order removing your spouse from the home and granting you temporary custody of the children. In that event, restraining orders are frequently used to provide some protection in the absence of the order of protection.

7.6 My spouse has never been violent, but I know he is going to be really angry and upset when the divorce papers are served. Do I need an order of protection?

An order of protection may not be appropriate today, but circumstances may change after you file for the divorce. You can obtain an order of protection at any time—before, during, or after the divorce. In the meantime, when a case is filed and a summons is served, an *automatic stay* restrains "both parties from physically abusing, harassing, intimidating, striking, or interfering with the personal liberty of the other party or the minor children of either party." The restraint also applies to removing children from the state or concealing them. The automatic stay is a court order and enforceable if violated. It does not have the same level of protection as an order of protection, though. An order of protection is a superior way to protect yourself.

7.7 My spouse says that I am crazy, that I am a liar, and that no judge will ever believe me if I tell the truth about the abusive behavior. What can I do if I don't have any proof?

You are not alone. It is very common for persons who abuse others to claim that their victims are liars and to make intimidating statements to discourage disclosure of the abuse. This is yet another form of abusive controlling behavior.

Domestic violence is usually silent; it rarely involves third-party witnesses. That is one reason it is so insidious. Often there is little physical evidence. However, even without physical evidence, a judge can enter orders to protect you and your children if you give truthful testimony about your abuse that the judge finds believable. Your testimony of the abuse is sufficient evidence.

Your attorney's skills and experience will support you to give effective testimony in the courtroom to establish your case. Let your lawyer know all of the facts and your concerns so that he or she can present your case persuasively based upon your experience.

7.8 I'm afraid my spouse is going to take all of the money out of the bank accounts and leave me with nothing. What can I do?

Talk to your attorney immediately. If you are worried about your spouse emptying financial accounts or selling marital assets, it is critical that you take action at once. Your attorney can advise you on your right to take possession of certain assets in order to protect them from being hidden or spent by your spouse.

Ask your lawyer about seeking a temporary restraining order. This order forbids your spouse from selling, transferring, hiding, or otherwise disposing of marital property before a final division of the property assets from your marriage is complete and the divorce is final. Under the appropriate circumstances, your attorney can obtain such an order as an emergency matter and without any advance notice to your spouse.

A *preliminary injunction* is another court order to prevent assets from "disappearing" before a divorce is final. It is much easier to prevent assets from disappearing than try to track them down later.

7.9 My spouse told me that if I ever file for divorce, I'll never see my child again. Can I stop this?

Your fear that your spouse will abduct your child is a common one. It can be helpful to look at some of the factors that appear to increase the risk that your child will be removed from the state by the other parent.

Many child abductions result from marriages that cross culture, race, religion, or ethnicity. A lower socioeconomic status, prior criminal record, and limited social or economic ties to the community can also increase risk. International abductions require money and resources and those with neither have a more difficult time fleeing with the child. Also, be aware that child abduction is considered a federal crime and the FBI, with their ample resources, will become involved in the event a parent wrongfully takes a child. Even though many intimidators threaten to kidnap children, implicitly or explicitly, experience shows that few act on the impulse.

When in doubt, try to secure your child's passport. You can also contact the U.S. Department of State at (888) 407-4747 and ask them about the State Department's Children's passport issuance alert program. Visit (http://travel.state.gov/abduction/abduction_580.html) for more information. Talk to your lawyer to assess the risks in your particular case. Together you can determine whether statements by your spouse are threats intended to control or intimidate you or whether legal action is needed to protect your child.

7.10 What legal steps can be taken to prevent my spouse from removing our child from the state?

We are a mobile society, and people frequently move after a divorce. If your spouse has indicated a desire to move with the children, he or she will need to get court permission to do so. A permanent move must be distinguished from a vacation. Your spouse may take the children for a vacation out of state without court permission as long as you have been advised of the itinerary and given contact information. If you are concerned about your child being improperly removed from the state, ask your lawyer whether any of these options might be available in your case:

- A court order giving you temporary physical possession of the children until the court conducts a custody hearing

- A court order denying your spouse permission to remove the child from the state

- A court order directing your spouse to turn over passports for the child and your spouse to the court

- The posting of a bond prior to your spouse exercising parenting time

- Supervised parenting time

Both state and federal laws are designed to avoid interstate gamesmanship and protect children from kidnapping. *The Uniform Child Custody Jurisdiction and Enforcement Act (UCCJEA)*, which is enforced in all states, was created to keep custody cases in the children's home state, where they have the most ties. *The Parental Kidnapping Prevention Act (PKPA)* makes it a federal crime for a parent to move a child out of state in violation of a valid custody order.

If you are concerned about your child being abducted, talk with your lawyer about all options available to you for your child's protection.

7.11 If either my spouse or I file for divorce, will my spouse have to leave the home?

Illinois law does not automatically require one of you to move from the marital residence when a case is filed. In fact, the law makes it difficult to remove your spouse from the home. To evict your spouse involuntarily, you must prove that you or the children are in danger as a result of your spouse continuing to live with you. Ordinarily this is difficult to prove and requires a full hearing, which may not be available for weeks or months due to the court's schedule. Of course, if domestic violence occurs, you may be eligible for an emergency order of protection, which will evict your spouse from the home immediately.

Sometimes your spouse's conduct, while annoying or unpleasant, doesn't rise to the level warranting their eviction. In that instance, judges sometimes create privacy zones within the home. For example, one of the spouses may be granted exclusive possession of an area of the house, such as the former master bedroom. If this type of order would help, check with your lawyer to see if it is available.

If cohabiting with your spouse is necessary and you are miserable, request that your lawyer use all efforts to move the process along as quickly as possible to conclude the divorce.

8

Parental Responsibility

For most parents, their child's welfare is a top priority when they start thinking about a divorce. Because of concerns about the children, many postpone divorce. Others determine that the emotional or economic costs of staying together outweigh those concerns. One thing is certain though: nearly everyone has anxiety about the effect of the divorce on his or her children.

Although most divorcing parents can agree on parenting issues, others cannot agree on much of anything. Through a variety of resources, courts attempt to protect your children to the fullest extent possible. Not surprisingly, when people lose sight of the best interest of the children and their fight becomes all-consuming, children suffer. For example, when a parent alienates the other parent or uses a child as a pawn for their own purposes, the child's security is sacrificed to the parent's need to fight.

It is vital to focus on the welfare of your children first and foremost. If possible, work together with your spouse to resolve parenting issues. Except in rare instances, children need to have a relationship with both parents. Divorce obviously impacts children's lives profoundly, but they can survive (and even thrive) after a divorce, if both parents work together, remain flexible and cooperative, and put their children's needs first.

8.1 What types of custody are available in Illinois?

Illinois no longer recognizes "child custody" as a legal designation. Our legislature determined that removing the term "custody" from the law will help parents focus on the interests of their children rather than seeking the "prize" of being designated the custodian of the children. Accordingly, we now refer to *allocation of parental responsibilities* and *parenting time.*

Now, rather than deciding who has the label of custodian, parents instead must try to develop a plan to divide time with their children. This doesn't mean that the children automatically live with each parent 50 percent of the time (although that is an option). The children may have one primary home base and have parenting time with the other parent. Additionally, the parents need to allocate time with the children on holidays, vacations and other special occasions.

The parents also need to determine which parent will decide issues related to the children's education, health care, religious training, and extracurricular activities. They can decide to make these decisions jointly or allocate responsibilities between themselves. For example, one parent might decide all educational and health-care issues while the other parent might decide issues of religious training. They then might jointly decide on extracurricular participation.

The parents are to develop a *parenting plan* jointly if possible. The attorneys will help the parties do this if necessary. Sometimes the parents can work it out on their own. Nobody knows children as well as their parents and they are in the best position to decide what type of arrangement will best serve the children's needs. If they can't agree on an arrangement they need to participate in mediation to try to come to an agreement.

The law requires a family court judge to monitor the parents' progress and if they can't come to an agreement within days of the filing of the case, each parent must present to the judge his or her proposed parenting plan. The judge then sets a hearing to determine issues of parenting time and allocation of parental responsibilities. Resolving parenting issues quickly helps give children closure and stability.

8.2 On what basis will the judge decide parenting time or decision-making rights?

Most people reach agreements regarding parenting time and decision-making rights. If you do reach an agreement and present an agreed parenting plan, your judge will need to approve it as being in the best interest of the children. If the judge disapproves, you will need to refine your plan in a way that satisfies the judge. If you can't reach an agreement, the judge will conduct a hearing to determine what arrangement best serves the needs of the children. The judge will hear testimony and review evidence regarding "the best interest of the child." In order to determine the best interest of the child, the judge will consider a number of factors, including:

The wishes of each parent. The judge will consider what both parents want, and their reasoning and opinions concerning what they believe will benefit their children. However, the court is not bound by the parents' stated preferences.

The wishes of the child, taking into account the child's maturity and ability to express reasoned and independent preferences as to parenting time. The wishes of older children who can articulate a preference will be considered. Generally, courts will start to consider the wishes of mature children starting at the age of twelve but a mature ten-year-old may influence the decision more than an immature sixteen-year-old who prefers the parent with fewer rules.

The child's adjustment to his home, school, and community. The judge will consider whether the children are thriving or struggling in their present environment.

The mental and physical health of all individuals involved. Obviously the physical or mental health of the parties impacts their ability to parent and should be considered by a judge. However, health problems are not usually determinative if they don't interfere with a parent's ability to care for the children.

The physical violence or threat of physical violence by the child's potential custodian, whether directed against the child or directed against another person. Here the court will consider whether either parent has behaved in an abusive manner to the other parent, the child, or any other person. The court will not only consider actual abuse, but threats and intimidation as well.

The occurrence of ongoing or related abuse as defined in Section 103 of the Illinois Domestic Violence Act of 1986, whether directed against the child or directed against another person. Section 103 of the *Domestic Violence Act* defines certain instances of conduct as abuse. The conduct under this Act is more expansive than physical abuse and includes harassment, intimidation of a dependent, interference with someone's personal liberty, stalking, and a variety of other offensive behaviors. The judge will hear evidence of either parent's conduct that falls within these categories.

The willingness and ability of each parent to facilitate and encourage a close and continuing relationship between the other parent and the child. Except in unusual circumstances, children thrive when they have a relationship with both parents. Children's identities derive from both parents, and therefore the law seeks to preserve both parents' relationships with the children. The judge will consider efforts by each parent to promote the children's relationship with the other parent.

Whether one of the parents is a sex offender. The court will consider whether one of the parents has a history or designation as a sex offender.

Other considerations. Courts will consider all factors affecting the best interest of the children, including past conduct of the parties related to parenting responsibilities. Judges will also consider distance between the parties' homes when determining both decision making and allocation of parenting time.

Judges often take an "If it ain't broken, don't fix it" approach to determining residential placement and decision making. If there is one parent who has primarily cared for the children and the children are doing well in that parent's care, judges often maintain the status quo. When both parents equally cared for the children, the task of determining residential arrangements becomes more challenging. Determining a child's future best interest inherently relies on each parent's past investment of time and attention to the children.

Courts will not consider parental behavior that does not affect their relationship with the children or impact their ability to parent. For example, if one of the parents smoked marijuana before the children were born, this conduct is irrelevant to their parenting time today and will not be considered. Although many parents attempt to question the other parent's character when it comes to deciding parenting time and decision making, much of that evidence would be deemed irrelevant and will be disregarded by the judge.

8.3   How can I prove that I was the primary caregiver?

One tool to assist you and your attorney in establishing your case as a past primary caregiver is a chart itemizing both parents' responsibilities for the child(ren). Consider the activities in the chart below to help you clarify your respective contributions as parents.

Parental Roles Chart

Activity	Parent 1	Parent 2
Attended prenatal medical visits		
Attended prenatal class		
Took time off work after child was born		
Got up with child for feedings		
Got up with child when sick at night		
Bathed child		
Put child to bed		
Potty-trained child		
Prepared and fed meals to child		
Helped child learn numbers, letters, colors		
Helped child with practice for music, dance lessons, sports		
Stayed home from work with sick child		
Took child to doctor visits		
Went to pharmacy for child's medication		
Administered child's medication		
Took child to therapy		
Took child to optometrist		
Took child to dentist		
Took child to get haircuts		

Parental Roles Chart (Continued)

Activity	Parent 1	Parent 2
Bought clothing for child		
Bought school supplies for child		
Transported child to school		
Picked child up after school		
Drove carpool for child's school		
Went to child's school activities		
Helped child with homework and projects		
Attended parent-teacher conferences		
Helped in child's classroom		
Chaperoned child's school trips and activities		
Transported child to day care		
Communicated with day care providers		
Attended day care activities		
Transported child from day care		
Signed child up for sports, dance, music		
Bought equipment for sports, dance, music		
Transported child to sports, dance, music		
Attended sports, dance, music		
Coached child's sports		
Transported child from sports, dance, music		
Knows child's friends and friends' families		
Took child to religious education		
Participated in child's religious education		
Obtained information and training about special needs of child		
Comforted child during times of emotional upset		

8.4   What's the difference between *visitation* and *parenting time*?

Illinois no longer recognizes the term *visitation*. The concept was abandoned when Illinois changed from a custody format to the allocation of parental time and responsibility. Traditionally, the time a noncustodial parent spent with the children was called *visitation*. Today, *parenting time* refers to the time a child spends with either parent.

8.5   If my spouse is awarded the majority of parenting time, how much time will I have with our child?

Parenting time schedules vary from case to case. As in all contests regarding children, the judge considers the "best interest" of the child in crafting an appropriate parenting schedule if the parents can't agree between themselves. Traditionally, non-residential parents had time with the child on alternate weekends and non-overnight time during the week. This traditional schedule has eroded over the past several years, permitting the nonresidential parent more time than before. Today it is more common to see weekend visits start Thursday after school and end Monday morning. Although some judges disallow overnight visits on school nights, most regularly allow overnight parenting time on non-school nights.

Some parents today are seeking and receiving approximately equal parenting time. This type of arrangement, of course, must be in the best interest of the children. Most frequently this schedule is permitted when both parents have a high level of involvement with the children and the parents live close to each other. Both parents must have a reasonably good level of communication with each other to facilitate this type of schedule. Sometimes, uninvolved parents seek this type of schedule either to obtain a reduction of child support or because they are emotionally distraught at the thought of losing daily contact with their children. Neither of these reasons is appropriate. The children's interests must always come first and trump the interests of either parent.

Among the factors affecting parenting time are the age and activities of the child(ren), the parents' work schedules, and the nature and extent of the parent's relationship with the child before the divorce. As an additional factor, the court will consider the child's need for consistency and regularity in their life. Most courts prefer not to make the child transition too many times during a given week.

If you and your spouse can reach an agreement about a parenting time schedule, you are likely to be more satisfied than if the judge imposes one. The two of you know your child's needs and your family traditions; you can better design a plan suited to your child. If you and your spouse are unable to reach an agreement on a parenting schedule, the judge will decide the schedule. Judges do their best to create a schedule permitting reasonable access to both parents, but judges don't always have enough insight regarding each child to craft a suitable schedule considering the needs of the child. You and your spouse should try to determine a schedule to avoid the unintended consequences of the judge, a stranger to the child, deciding the child's fate.

8.6 My spouse and I have agreed to each of us having the primary residence of one our children. Will the court permit this?

Remember that any agreement you and your spouse reach concerning the children must be approved by the judge. Although unorthodox, the judge may permit split residences if the circumstances are appropriate. For example, a fifteen-year-old boy may live with his father and his eight-year-old sister may live with her mother. Ordinarily, judges want assurances that the two siblings will see each other as frequently as possible. Although rare, if the judge considers it suitable, he or she may order split residences even if the parents don't agree.

8.7 May I get an order granting primary responsibility for the children before the conclusion of the case?

When necessary, the court can enter a temporary order allocating time and decision-making rights to a parent. If you and your spouse are amicable, such an order may be unnecessary as you and your spouse can informally work out appropriate arrangements pending the conclusion of the case. Where necessary, however, the court can enter orders allocating time, responsibilities, and any other order necessary to ensure the protection of the children.

If you and your spouse continue to reside together during the divorce, temporary parenting orders are is usually unnecessary, assuming the two of you can reach agreements concerning the children's day-to-day welfare. If disagreements develop, ask your lawyer about the possibility of a temporary court order. Also understand that if you move out, you are not permitted to automatically take the children with you. If possible, discuss this issue with your spouse before making final decisions to leave the marital residence. Also notify your lawyer in advance of any move in order to understand the repercussions on the parenting issues.

Due to time constraints, it is not unusual for a court to deny feuding couples a right to a temporary hearing. Judges reason that the same facts heard at a temporary hearing will be presented at a final parental allocation hearing and therefore it is inefficient to conduct two full hearings on the subject. Instead, judges will frequently put these cases on a "fast track" in order to resolve the entire case, including allocation of parenting time and decision making as soon as possible. Sometimes judges look for other interim solutions if you and your spouse disagree on temporary parenting arrangements. For example, the court may order a "nesting arrangement" that involves the children remaining at home and the parents moving out of the home at set intervals. Discuss your options with your lawyer if you anticipate the need for a temporary parenting order.

8.8 Do I have to let my spouse see the children before I am required by a court order?

Unless your children are at risk, they should maintain regular contact with the other parent. It is important for children to experience the presence of both parents in their lives, regardless of their parents' separation. Even if there is no temporary order for parenting time, cooperate with your spouse to provide reasonable time with your children. But when a parent may endanger the children, that parent's access should be limited; in that event, contact your lawyer about appropriate protection orders.

Regardless of whether you consider your spouse an inadequate parent, work with him or her to establish reasonable parenting time unless there are real concerns about the children's safety or welfare. If you deny contact with the other parent, your judge may question whether you have the best interest of your child at heart. And arguments that "the kids don't want to see him" are rarely persuasive. Your willingness to promote the other parent's relationship is a factor that the court will consider in a contested trial.

On the other hand, if your spouse makes demands for time that you consider excessive or disruptive to the children, don't automatically agree either. Talk to your lawyer about an appropriate temporary parenting schedule. Balance the children's needs to see the other parent with their need for stability.

8.9   I am seeing a therapist. Will that hurt my case?

Talk with your lawyer about the implications of therapy. It may be that what sent you to therapy doesn't affect your child or your ability to be a loving and supportive parent. Seeking help from a therapist during a difficult time is laudatory, not a stigma. Your emotional well-being makes you a better parent. Most judges understand the emotional challenges of a divorce and don't hold therapy against anyone.

Be aware, however, that your spouse's lawyer may try to obtain your mental health records. Although Illinois law makes it very difficult to obtain these records, the possibility exists. Generally, however, the benefits of therapy far outweigh the risks that your therapy will hurt you in court.

8.10   Can having a live-in partner hurt my chances of receiving parenting time and decision-making rights?

If you want to live with your boyfriend or girlfriend, discuss the consequences with your attorney first. This decision may seriously affect your case. If you are already living with someone, let your attorney know right away. Generally, it is a bad idea. Focus on getting your divorce concluded before entering into new relationships. The distraction of a new relationship may cloud your judgment when you have to make decisions that will last for a lifetime. Also, your pursuit of a new relationship during this delicate time for your children may overwhelm and confuse them.

8.11   Will the children be exposed to details of the divorce?

Although most parents try to shelter their children from the conflict, some parents use poor judgment. These misguided parents talk to the children about the details of the case or share court documents with them. This behavior usually displeases judges who will enter restraining orders restricting either parent from revealing any details to the children. If your spouse is talking to the children about the case or talking negatively about you, speak with your attorney about your options. It might be a good idea to seek court-ordered counseling for the children to try to counter your spouse's negative behavior.

Parents who share information with the children under the pretense, "I am not going to lie to my children," are fooling themselves, if not being outright dishonest. There is a difference between lying to the children and being discreet for the sake of their emotional welfare. White lies that protect the children are acceptable and good common sense.

Parents who use their children as confidants also hurt the children. Even though everyone needs a friend and confidant during a difficult period in his or her life, don't make your child that person. You don't help your children by placing them in that role. During a period when there is much upheaval for children, they need the guidance and protection of a parent who knows when to say no. And it is much harder to say no to a friend. Don't give up your parenting responsibilities during this difficult time.

Even if your spouse has mistreated you, it is rare that the disclosure of the mistreatment will in any way benefit the children. The children need a relationship with both of you. They need the security of knowing that it is okay to love both of you. When you rage to the children about your spouse, it inhibits the children from expressing their love for the other parent. Put your feelings aside for the best interest of your children.

8.12   My spouse told me that she is going to have the children sit in the trial and watch. Is this possible?

Probably not. Judges try to protect children from the conflict of their parents and virtually all will bar the children from the courtroom. Judges recognize the harm this would cause the children, even if your spouse doesn't understand this.

8.13   Should I hire a private investigator to prove my spouse is having an affair?

It depends. Under Illinois law, proof of the affair itself is usually unimportant; the important thing is how your spouse's behavior affects his or her ability to parent. But sometimes, to get psychological closure, particularly when your spouse repeatedly denies having an extramarital relationship, confirmation that he or she is indeed having an affair will help you emotionally move on. In that event, speak with your attorney about the costs and details for using a private investigator.

8.14   Will the fact that I had an affair during the marriage hurt my chances of being with my children?

The fact that you had an affair will not by itself disqualify you from parenting time or decision-making rights. The standard for the court to consider is the best interest of the children, not whether you were a loyal spouse. If the affair did not impact your ability to parent, or did not affect the children, it will likely be unimportant to the issues related to the children. If, on the other hand, the children were exposed to the affair, or your parenting was affected by the affair (such as missing events for the children or neglecting them emotionally), the issue may impact the case.

8.15   During the months it takes to get a divorce, is it okay to date or will it hurt my chances for increased parenting time and decision-making rights?

If contested parenting issues exist, talk with your attorney about your plans to begin dating. Dating may be irrelevant if the children are unaware. However, most judges will frown upon you exposing the children to your new relationship when they are still adjusting to the separation of their parents. Even though you may be excited about a new romantic interest and want your children to meet this person, it is unnecessary, and potentially harmful for your children. Plus, if your spouse discovers that the children have met this new person in your life, it may inflame an already volatile situation. For the sake of your children and your own interests, try to keep things as calm as possible during this difficult period. Taunting a spouse by flaunting a new relationship may turn a cooperative case into a nasty holy war. Be careful and discreet.

If your spouse is challenging your parental rights, it may be best to focus your energy on your children, the litigation, and taking care of yourself. There will be plenty of time for a new relationship after the case concludes.

8.16 I'm gay and came out to my spouse when I filed for divorce. What impact will my sexual orientation have on my case for parenting time and decision-making rights?

Illinois law does not limit your rights as a parent based upon your sexual orientation. Your sexual orientation itself is unimportant; what's important is how your sexuality impacts the children. Assuming your lifestyle does not disrupt the children, it should make no difference in the case. You may want to speak with a child psychologist about the best way to approach this issue with your children.

Although you may be excited about finally revealing your true nature, this revelation may be devastating to your spouse. Be sensitive and patient, and don't be indignant with him or her for failing to immediately embrace the new you. Consider his or her feelings. You may have struggled with the decision to come out for years, but your spouse now must immediately contend with its implications, which may be difficult for him or her.

8.17 Can I have witnesses provide information on my behalf?

Witnesses are critical in most cases. This is particularly true in contested cases involving children. It is important to determine early which witnesses may help bolster your claims. Witnesses assist even before trial: they may speak with the guardian *ad litem* and other court investigators about your strengths as a parent and any problems with your spouse's parenting. The best witnesses are those who don't have any bias. You could use your mother to testify about how wonderful you are, but a better witness would be one of the children's teachers, or day care providers, who are more impartial about each parent's relative parenting qualities. Generally, the judge wants to know more about concrete issues such as parenting strengths and weaknesses rather than more-abstract character issues.

In considering which witnesses would best support your case, your attorney may consider the following:

- Does the witness have any alignment to either you or your spouse? Are they biased?

- What is the relationship of the witness to the child and the parents?

- What has been this witness's opportunity to observe you or the other parent, especially with your child? How frequently? How recently?

- How long has the witness known you or the other parent?

- Has the witness made inconsistent statements concerning any of the issues he or she will testify about?

- Does this witness have knowledge different from that of other witnesses?

- Is the witness available and willing to testify?

- Will this person be an effective witness? Will they be clear in conveying information?

- Is the witness credible? Will the judge believe this witness?

You and your attorney should work together to determine which witnesses would best support your case. Provide your attorney with a list of potential witnesses as soon as you determine that parenting issues will not likely be resolved by agreement.

Give your attorney the phone number, e-mail address, and workplace of each of your potential witnesses. This information will save your attorney time when arranging interviews and notifying the witnesses about court appearances. When parents give conflicting testimony during a custody trial, the testimony of other witnesses can be the key to determining the outcome of the case.

8.18 I contacted a witness who has helpful information, but she told me she won't agree to testify. Can I force her to testify?

If a witness lives in Illinois, you can issue a subpoena, which forces the witness to appear at a designated court hearing or deposition. Even with a subpoena, some witnesses may refuse to testify based upon privileges. A *privilege* exempts someone from having to testify. For example, a doctor-and-patient relationship is considered privileged. The law wants patients to have the ability to speak freely with a doctor without fear of their statements being disclosed. The privilege permits the doctor to refuse to testify about statements made by the patient under certain circumstances.

In general, be careful with reluctant witnesses. If an involuntary witness gets subpoenaed, the person's memory may mysteriously fade or, worse yet, he or she may become hostile and passive-aggressive, providing helpful testimony for the other side. Discuss with your lawyer the pros and cons of having a reluctant witness subpoenaed in your case.

8.19 How old do the children have to be before they can speak to the judge?

The judge will determine whether to interview the children regarding their preferences or concerns. In addition to the age of a child, a judge may consider the child's maturity and personality. Generally, judges don't meet with very young children who can't express their opinions.

If either you or your spouse wants the judge to interview your child, you can request that the judge speak with the child in the judge's office (chambers) rather than from the witness stand. This interview is known as an *in camera interview.* In the event a guardian *ad litem* or child representative has been appointed in your case, that person will also be present during the interview. The attorneys may also be present. If both attorneys agree, they can waive their appearance so the child feels more comfortable disclosing their feelings without their parents' representatives sitting across the table from them.

If the attorneys do appear at the interview, it is unlikely they will be permitted to question the child. Occasionally, judges permit the attorneys to ask questions but this is the exception. More customarily, judges allow the attorneys to write out potential questions in advance and submit them to the judge to consider. The rules also require the discussion with the child be in the presence of a court reporter.

Before asking for such an interview, remember the anxiety this will likely cause your child. Some children will be terrified. For others, the process may be therapeutic. Each child is different so make sure to consider the impact this process will have on your child.

8.20   Will my attorney want to speak with my child?

In most instances the attorney won't need to speak with the child. However, if you have a parenting dispute or claims of abuse or neglect, the attorney may want to interview the child directly. As a general rule, try to exclude your children from the case. Don't volunteer him or her as a witness to corroborate your version of events unless it is absolutely necessary and the attorney feels their testimony is vital. Ask your attorney about the goal of the interview before you agree to an interview of your child. Most attorneys are not trained to interview children, especially younger children. If the attorney has not spent a lot of time with children or is not familiar with child development, the interview may not provide meaningful information.

If your attorney asks to meet with your child, provide some background information. Let your attorney know your child's personality, some of his or her interests, and any topics that might upset your child. This background will help the attorney exercise necessary care during the interview. If you are concerned that going to your attorney's office will cause undue anxiety for your child, ask your attorney whether the interview can take place in a setting that would be more comfortable for your child. This might be a public place or your home.

8.21   What is the role of a guardian *ad litem* or child representative?

When parents have a family law conflict, Illinois law provides three advocates for children: a guardian *ad litem,* a child representative, or a traditional attorney. All three are resources for children, but their roles differ.

The guardian *ad litem* sometimes referred to as the (*GAL*) is a specially trained attorney who investigates the pending issues. The GAL prepares a report concerning contested parenting issues or any other issue affecting the child's best interest. Frequently, the GAL is asked to make recommendations for the judge concerning residential arrangements, decision making, and parenting time. The GAL may be asked to testify by you or your spouse and may be cross-examined by either parent's attorney. The guardian *ad litem's* role is primarily as a court investigator and witness concerning the best interest of the child. The GAL advocates for what he or she believes is in the child's best interest, rather than what the child wants. Although the GAL will consider the child's preferences, they do not bind him or her.

A *child representative* is also a specially trained attorney. The child representative advocates for the best interest of the child in court. Like the guardian *ad litem,* the child representative investigates the issues. But the child representative may not render an opinion or recommendation, or testify concerning the best interest of the children. Instead, the child representative offers legal arguments to the court based upon the evidence presented at trial. Distinguished from the guardian *ad litem,* the role of a child representative is more akin to a lawyer advocating the best interest of the children rather than as a witness expressing opinions on the subject.

A third option, rarely used, is the appointment of a *traditional attorney* to represent the child. The attorney for the child advocates for the child the same way a lawyer does for an adult client. The lawyer can file pleadings and argue on behalf of the child. Unlike a guardian *ad litem* or a child representative, the attorney advocates based upon the child's wishes, rather than upon the child's best interest.

Ask your attorney about the relative advantages of having a guardian *ad litem* versus a child representative. Also ask when it would be appropriate to seek a traditional lawyer for your child. Regardless, remember that you and your spouse will be responsible for the costs of their services. Get an estimate from your lawyer concerning the expected costs of any of these options.

8.22   What is typically included in a *parenting plan*?

A *parenting plan* is a document detailing how you and your spouse will parent after the divorce. It sets forth your respective rights and responsibilities with regard to your children. Among the issues addressed in a parenting agreement are:

- Allocation of decision-making responsibilities
- Provisions for the child(ren)'s living arrangement and parenting time with each parent
- A mediation provision if decision making is to be made jointly
- Provisions regarding access to medical and other records
- Which parent has the majority of time
- The child(ren)'s address for school enrollment purposes
- Contact information for each parent
- Written notification procedures in the event either parent later seeks to relocate his or her residence
- Notification protocol in the event of emergencies, health care, travel, or other child-related issues
- Transportation arrangements between the parents
- Communication provisions for each parent when the child is with the other parent
- Provisions for resolving in advance any issues of future relocation by either parent
- Provisions for future modification in the event that certain contingencies occur
- Provisions for a right of first refusal when parents cannot be with the child
- Any other appropriate arrangements to facilitate the cooperation of the parents.

Detailed parenting plans provide clarity regarding each parent's rights and responsibilities. These agreements also provide security for the child by reducing parental conflict, which lowers the risk of returning to court. Anything that reduces parental conflict ultimately benefits the child.

8.23 I don't think it's safe for my children to have any contact with my spouse. What are my options?

First, be aware that the law imposes a strict burden on a parent seeking to restrict the other parent's access to the children. The law presumes it is in the best interest of children to have a substantial relationship with both parents. In order to limit your spouse's access to the children, you must prove that the children will be "seriously endangered" if protections are not implemented. Convincing evidence is necessary to restrict another parent's access to the children.

The type of evidence that would support a finding of "serious endangerment" would be concrete examples of past abuse or neglect. Vague or intuitive concerns about child safety would not be sufficient to limit access; you must present definite proof to support the concern. Therefore, make sure to log all incidents supporting claims of unfitness. Make your log available to your lawyer so the lawyer can evaluate the strength of your claims.

Assuming you have sufficient evidence to support your concern about the children's safety, the judge has a number of remedies. The judge might order supervised parenting time. Supervised parenting time allows the other parent to exercise his or her parenting time under the supervision of another person. This procedure allows the parent access to the children while ensuring the safety of the children.

Sometimes the supervisor is a professional social worker and other times he or she is a trusted friend or family member. Usually this procedure is short term, designed to protect the children while the other parent's relationship is rehabilitated. Another option is for the judge to suspend all parenting time until a guardian *ad litem* or court-appointed psychologist determines the nature of the problem between the parent and the children. Finally, the court may start allowing the children small amounts of time with the other parent and increase it incrementally as the children feel more comfortable.

The court may also consider the following:

- Exchanges of the children in a public place
- Parenting classes
- Anger management or other therapy
- Prohibitions against the parent drinking alcohol when the children are present or an alcohol monitoring system

Judges have different approaches where children are at risk. Recognize that there are also practical considerations, such as cost or the availability of people to supervise visits.

8.24 My spouse keeps saying he'll get the children because there were no witnesses to his abuse and I can't prove it. Is he right?

No. In this case, your spouse is a bully. These types of statements are just another form of abuse; and the abuser uses them to intimidate or control you. Most domestic violence is behind closed doors and judges know this. If you have been a victim of abusive behavior by your spouse, or if you have witnessed your children as victims, your testimony is likely to be the most compelling evidence.

Be sure to tell your attorney about anyone who may have either seen your spouse's behavior or spoken to you or your children right after an abusive incident. They may be important witnesses when determining parental time and decision-making rights. Fighting back is the best way to neutralize a bully.

8.25 I am concerned about protecting my child from abuse by my spouse. Which types of past abuse by my spouse are important to tell my attorney?

Your attorney should be given a full history of your spouse's behavioral problems. Some examples would include:

- Hitting, kicking, pushing, shoving, or slapping your or your child
- Sexual abuse
- Threats to harm you or the child
- Threats to abduct your child

- Suicide threats
- Alcohol or drug abuse
- Possession of firearms
- Destruction of property
- Torture of pets or harm to them
- Requiring your child to keep secrets

The process of writing down past events may help you to remember other incidents of abuse that you had forgotten. Be as complete as possible.

8.26 What documents or items should I give my attorney to help prove the history of domestic violence by my spouse?

The following may be useful exhibits if your parental responsibility case goes to court:

- Photographs of injuries
- Photographs of damaged property
- Abusive or threatening notes, letters, or e-mails
- Abusive or threatening voice or text messages
- Your journal entries about abuse
- Police reports
- Medical records
- Court records
- Criminal and traffic records
- Damaged property, such as torn clothing

Tell your attorney which of these you have or are able to obtain. Ask your lawyer whether others can be acquired through a subpoena or other means.

8.27 I had a great relationship with my children prior to the divorce. Now they won't even speak with me. What's going on?

Parental alienation is, unfortunately, all too common in family court. There is some controversy about this topic, but it is undeniable that some parents actively discourage the other parent's relationship with the children. The one thing you can't do is to ignore this behavior. If you do nothing, there is a reasonable chance the alienating parent will succeed.

Generally, if you had a good bond with the children prior to the divorce, it is rare the children will remain alienated long term. Usually, after initial reluctance to maintain the relationship, children come around. Balance is the key to addressing this problem. Pushing too hard may backfire, and writing the children off would be tragic. In the extreme case, drastic action may be necessary, including removing the children from the alienating parent. Develop a strategy with your lawyer to manage this problem. Consult with a clinical psychologist to determine the best way to proceed, considering your personal family dynamics.

8.28   I want to talk to my spouse about our child(ren), but all she wants to do is argue. How can I communicate without it always turning into a fight?

Because conflict is high between you and your spouse, consider the following:

- Ask your lawyer to help you get a court order for parenting time that is specific and detailed. This lowers the amount of necessary communication between you and your spouse.

- Put as much information in writing as possible.

- Consider using Internet resources such as (www.Ourfamilywizard.com)

- Consider using e-mail, mail, or fax, especially for less urgent communication.

- Avoid criticisms of your spouse's parenting.

- Avoid telling your spouse how to parent.

- Be factual and businesslike.

- Acknowledge to your spouse their good parental qualities, such as being concerned, attentive, or generous.

- Keep your child out of any conflicts.

You can only control your own behavior. By focusing on yourself and how you respond to your spouse, conflict has the potential to decrease.

8.29 What if the child is not returned from parenting time at the agreed-upon time? Should I call the police?

Calling the police should be done only as a last resort if you feel that your child is at risk for abuse or neglect, or if your attorney has advised you that such a call is warranted. The involvement of law enforcement officials in parental conflict can result in far greater trauma to a child than a late return at the end of a parenting time.

The appropriate response to a child being returned late depends upon the circumstances. If the problem is a recurring one, talk to your lawyer regarding your options. It may be that a change in the schedule would be in the best interest of your child. Or perhaps you could pick up the child at the end of the other parent's time. Regardless of the behavior of the other parent, make every effort to keep your child out of any conflicts between the adults.

8.30 My ex refuses to turn over the children for my time with them. What can I do about it?

First, discuss the matter with your attorney. He or she can bring appropriate petitions to enforce court orders and punish violations. In the event one party violates an order of court "without substantial cause or justification," the party who violates the order must pay the other side's fees. Also, the court may order make-up parenting time for the time missed. Ultimately, if this behavior is chronic, the judge has the power to limit the other parent's time with the children.

The law also provides a criminal remedy. Statute 720 ILCS 5/10-5.5 is the Illinois "Unlawful Visitation or Parenting Time Interference" statute. Violations of this statute are considered petty offenses, but after two convictions, the third offense is a Class A misdemeanor with penalties of jail time. Responsible reports should be filed when these types of problems arise. Don't use the criminal law as a sword. The family court judge will frown upon petty criminal complaints used to harass your ex-spouse.

8.31   If I have the majority of parenting time, may I relocate without the permission of the court?

It depends. Parents residing in Cook, DuPage, Kane, Lake, McHenry, and Will counties may relocate up to twenty-five miles from their current home without permission of the other parent or the court. Parents residing in all other counties in the state may move up to fifty miles without permission. Any moves beyond those distance limitations need permission to relocate either the other parent or from the court.

If a parent with the majority of parenting time intends to relocate beyond the radius limitations, that parent must give the other parent notice at the earliest possible date, and the judge may consider a parent's failure to give notice in determining the good faith of the move. If the other parent, after being given notice, agrees to the move, the parenting plan will need to be modified to reflect the changed residence. If the nonmoving parent objects to the relocation, the court will conduct a hearing to determine if the relocation with the children will be permitted. Although either parent is always free to relocate anywhere in the world, the question is whether the court will allow the children to accompany him or her. In determining whether to allow the relocation, the judge is to consider the following factors:

- The circumstances and reasons for the intended relocation

- The reasons, if any, why a parent is objecting to the intended relocation

- The history and quality of each parent's relationship with the child and specifically whether a parent has substantially failed or refused to exercise the parental responsibilities allocated to him or her under the parenting plan or allocation judgment

- The educational opportunities for the child at the existing location and at the proposed new location

- The presence or absence of extended family at the existing location and at the proposed new location

- The anticipated impact of the relocation on the child

- Whether the court will be able to fashion a reasonable allocation of parental responsibilities between parents if the relocation occurs

- The wishes of the child, taking into account the child's maturity and ability to express reasoned and independent preferences as to relocation

- Possible arrangements for the exercise of parental responsibilities appropriate to the parents' resources and circumstances and the developmental level of the child

- Minimization of the impairment to a parent-child relationship caused by a parent's relocation

- Any other relevant factors bearing on the child's best interest

Court permission is only required for a parent with equal or the majority of parenting time. A parent with less than the majority of time is free to move anywhere and a new parenting schedule will need to be determined. This provision is a relatively new law. Formerly a parent was free to move anywhere in the state and only needed court permission to move outside of Illinois. Now a parent can move outside of Illinois without permission as long as the relocation does not exceed the mileage limitations discussed above.

8.32 What information should I collect to improve my chances of success if I am seeking to move with the children?

Gather evidence supporting the reason for the move. For example, if the basis of the move is a job transfer, collect employment records establishing the need to move. Also, provide pictures showing your prospective home and community. Gather information about the school the children will attend, extracurricular and cultural activities available to them, and other benefits of the area they will relocate to. Also, since the judge will weigh the move against the impact to the other parent, develop a proposed replacement parenting time schedule that will, to the extent possible, provide substantial parenting time for the noncustodial parent.

8.33 For years my ex-spouse has threatened to take my children to another state to be closer to his or her parents. What can I do to increase my chances of blocking the move?

The single best way to enhance your chances of success is to maintain a substantial relationship with the children. In addition to exercising all of your parenting time, attend all school events, coach your children's activities, and generally take an active interest in their lives. If you are very involved with your children, your ex-spouse will have a more difficult time successfully removing the children from the state.

8.34 After the divorce, can I legally take our children out of the state or country during my parenting time?

Ordinarily, either parent may temporarily remove the children from the state (or country) for a vacation or other reason, such as a family reunion. Before leaving, the traveling parent must inform the other parent of their itinerary and contact information. International travel often requires consent by the other parent. If you anticipate that your ex-spouse will be uncooperative, contact your attorney as soon as the travel dates are set, in order to give your attorney plenty of time in case you need court action to force compliance.

8.35 If I am not given parental decision-making rights, what rights do I have regarding medical records and medical treatment for my child?

Regardless of which parent has been allocated decision-making rights, state law allows both parents to have access to the medical records of their children and to make emergency medical decisions. Make sure you are listed as a parent with the children's physician, in order to access reports regarding the child's health.

8.36 If I am not allocated decision-making rights for my child's education, how will I know what's going on at my child's school? What rights to records do I have there?

Regardless of your decision-making rights, you have access to your child's school records. Develop a relationship with your child's teachers and the school staff. Request to be put on the school's mailing list for all notices. Find out what is necessary for you to do to get copies of important school information and report cards.

Set aside any acrimony you feel for your spouse. Attempt to communicate, both to share and to receive information about your child's progress in school. This will enable you to support your child and one another during challenging periods of your child's education. Working together also provides the child a sense of security; your ability to put aside your own issues for the sake of the child communicates your concern and love.

Regardless of which parent is allocated decision-making rights, your child will benefit by both parents' involvement in his or her education through participation in parent-teacher conferences, attendance at school events, help with school homework, and positive communication with each other.

8.37 What can I do if my child does not want to go for his or her parenting time?

One of the most perplexing problems in family court is the child who does not want to spend time with the other parent. One parent claims the child doesn't want to go because the other parent doesn't engage the child, or otherwise mistreats the child. The other parent argues that the favored parent has alienated the child, and has negatively influenced the relationship. Sometimes both parents are correct. In considering this dilemma, judges look to the following:

- What is the child's stated reason for not wanting to go?

- Does the child appear afraid, anxious, or sad?

- Have any legitimate safety issues been disclosed?

- Has there been a history of interference by the favored parent?

- Does the favored parent prepare the child for time with the other parent by speaking about the experience with enthusiasm and encouragement?

- Is the child perceiving the favored parent's anxiety about the situation and mirroring that anxiety?

- Has the favored parent consciously or subconsciously subverted the child's transition to the other home by engaging in fun activities with the child just before the pickup?

- Has the estranged parent made the parenting time fun and nonthreatening by engaging in activities rather than plunking the child down in front of a television for the weekend?

Children deserve to have a relationship with both parents, regardless of any mistrust between the parents. Parents need to set aside their anxiety and encourage the children to enjoy time with the other parent. The estranged parent must be patient and understand the children's natural aversion to changes to their day-to-day routine. Each child is different, and a cooperative approach is best. When both parents work together to soothe their children, these issues rarely last.

Unfortunately, people often lose sight of their children's interest as they become overwhelmed by their personal domestic dramas. Then a judge must get involved. Judges treat compliance with court orders for parenting time seriously. If a judge believes that one parent is intentionally interfering with the other's parenting time or the parent-child relationship, it can result in further litigation and ultimately in a loss of rights. At the same time, judges want to ensure that children are safe. Talk with your attorney about the best approach in your situation.

8.38 What steps can I take to prevent my spouse from getting our child in the event of my death?

Unless the other parent is unfit, he or she will have first priority as the guardian of your child in the event of your death. Many people have wills naming desired guardians in the event of his or her death. It is helpful to state your preference, but a will does not override a fit parent's right to care for his or her child.

8.39   My spouse claims that his parents have parenting time rights in addition to his parenting time. Is this correct?

No. Grandparents only have independent rights to seek court-ordered time with the children if one of the parents is deceased and then only under limited circumstances.

For updates on topics in this chapter visit (www.peskindlaw.com/legal-updates).

9

Child Support

Formerly, Illinois determined child support based on the net income of the noncustodial parent. That formula placed Illinois in the minority of states. Most states already considered the income of both parents when calculating child support. Illinois recently joined the dual-income states by adopting legislation reflecting an "income share" model for determining child support.

The new child support laws calculate "child support based upon the parents' combined adjusted net income estimated to have been allocated to the child if the parents and children were living in an intact household" (750 ILCS 5/505). This means that support is intended to approximate the expenses the parents would have incurred for the children had they not divorced.

The Illinois Department of Healthcare and Family Services (HFS) has developed economic tables reflecting assumed expenses for raising children in an intact household, and a calculator allowing a simplified calculation of support based upon ratios of the combined net incomes of the parents. The tables are set forth at the State of Illinois HFS website that can be found at (www.illinois.gov/hfs/SiteCollectionDocuments/ IncomeSharesScheduleBasedonNetIncome.pdf). Not only is a trial court to consider both parents' incomes, the court is also to consider the child's physical care arrangements. In other words, the parenting schedule will affect the amount of child support.

After the amount of the total support is allocated between the parents based upon their incomes and parenting time, one

Child Support

of the parents may be required to pay the other parent an offset. For example, if based upon the ratio of the parents' combined net incomes, one parent's net income is 70 percent of the total, he or she will owe the other parent 70 percent of the support amount as determined by the HFS tables.

More information is available at the State of Illinois HFS website at (www.illinois.gov/hfs/childsupport/Pages/default. aspx).

9.1   How much child support am I entitled to?

Unlike the former child support law, which made determining child support relatively straightforward, more steps are involved in determining support now. Just as with the former child support law, courts are to apply the new guidelines in most cases. A court may opt out of the guidelines if it finds that application of the guidelines is not in the child's best interest. Assuming the guidelines apply, the first step to determine child support is to look at both parents' gross incomes. The next step is to determine the parents' respective net incomes using either a standardized tax rate or the parents' actual tax rate. After those net incomes are determined, they are combined.

So if, for example, the combined net income of the parents is $150,000, the support will be based on the amount of money parents in intact households of $150,000 spend on their children. Those sums can be found in tables published by the State of Illinois Department of Healthcare and Family Services, which reflect total support owed by the parents. That support amount is then allocated between the parents based upon ratios of their combined net income, with certain adjustments based upon allocation of time. An online child support calculator is available at (www.illinois.gov/hfs/ChildSupport/parents/ Pages/ChildSupportEstimator.aspx).

9.2   What are some circumstances when the judge might deviate from the guidelines?

Illinois child support guidelines ordinarily apply for families with combined gross income of $500,000 or less. Although guidelines are to be used for all temporary, permanent, or modification proceedings involving child support, the court may deviate from the guidelines if their use would be "inequitable, unjust, or inappropriate." In determining whether to deviate, the court must set forth its reasons and the proper amount of support if guidelines are applied. In determining whether to deviate, the judge may consider:

- Extraordinary medical expenditures necessary to preserve the life or health of either party or their children

- Additional expenses for a child who has special medical, physical, or developmental needs

- Any other appropriate factor affecting the best interest of a child

Where the combined adjusted gross income of the parents exceeds $500,000, the court may use its discretion in setting support. The support is not to be less than the amounts to be paid for the highest level of adjusted gross income published in the HFS schedule.

9.3   How is gross income determined?

For child support purposes, gross income includes "the total of all income from all sources," subject to the following exceptions:

- Public assistance benefits including temporary assistance to needy families, Social Security income, and the Supplemental Nutrition Assistance program

- Benefits and income received by the parent for other children in the household

The total of all income includes base pay, overtime, bonuses, business income, and under certain circumstances gifts from family members. Income is not limited just to base wages.

If the parent is disabled or retired, gross income is to include Social Security benefits and retirement benefits paid for the benefit of the child in calculating that parent's gross income. The parent receiving those benefits is entitled, however, to a child support credit for the amount of benefits paid to the other parent. Spousal support or maintenance received according to a court order is to be included in the recipient's gross income as well.

Under certain circumstances, there are to be adjustments to gross or net income when computing support:

Court-ordered support. If a parent has a court ordered child support obligation for a child from a different relationship who is not subject to the present proceeding, the amount of support actually paid for that child (or children) is to be deducted from the net income of the paying parent.

Non-court-ordered support. With regard to non-court-ordered support for other children, the parent paying the support can deduct from his or her gross income the *lesser* of sums actually paid to support the other child (whether in the household or not) or 75 percent of the amount of guideline child support that parent would pay for the other child.

Maintenance. Court-ordered maintenance to a spouse in the same proceeding or from another relationship is deductible from the gross income of the spouse ordered to pay the maintenance.

9.4 After gross income is determined, how do the courts determine net income for the purposes of determining child support?

Child support is based upon the net income of both parties. *Net income* is defined as gross income minus taxes. Taxes are to be determined either by using a *standardized tax amount* or an *individualized tax amount.* The court is to use the standardized tax amount except under the following circumstances:

- Where the parties agree to calculate taxes based on an individualized amount

- If the court conducts a summary hearing under Section 501 and an "eligible" party opts in to the individual computation method

- Where child support is determined in an evidentiary hearing. Under this circumstance the individualized tax amount is to be determined based upon the record established.

9.5   My ex-spouse's gross income can't be determined because he has a cash business and doesn't disclose all of the income. How will the judge address that problem?

It's not uncommon for a parent to make this claim but he or she will need some proof to substantiate it. Did the family lifestyle exceed the declared income? For example, did the family take expensive vacations despite showing income of $20,000 per year? Assuming the judge believes that income is not properly disclosed, the judge can impute income to either parent, that is, the judge will determine what he or she thinks that parent is making or should be making and apply the guidelines using that amount. Alternatively, the judge is authorized to determine a reasonable amount of support considering the needs of the children and their standard of living prior to the divorce.

9.6   My income frequently goes up and down, depending upon commissions and bonuses. How will the judge deal with that type of variable income?

Generally, there are two ways of dealing with this scenario. First, the judge may average your total income over a three- or four-year period and determine an annual average and apply the guidelines to the net of that figure. Alternatively, the judge may set support based on your base income only and then if you receive additional bonus income, you would pay a predetermined percentage of additional income received at that time. This latter type of arrangement would require you to provide proof of the additional income when you receive it as well as tax returns in order to verify that the appropriate amount was paid throughout the year.

9.7   If the court orders me to pay based on the guidelines, I won't have enough money to live on. Are there any exceptions to these guidelines?

The judge can disregard the guidelines if he or she determines they are inappropriate. A judge may order support at a rate above or below the guidelines when appropriate. In order to have the judge deviate from the guidelines, you will need to show not only financial hardship for yourself, but that the children have sufficient resources through the other parent so that a reduced payment will not harm them.

9.8 I feel bad for my ex-spouse and will agree not to accept any child support. Is this acceptable?

People often feel sympathy for someone going through a hard time, particularly someone they once loved. The judge will not usually permit a parent to waive child support, however. Support is considered the independent benefit of the child and the law provides that you cannot waive the benefit of another, even your child. However, if your income is significant and you can prove the child will be well provided for, it is possible that the judge may approve this type of arrangement. Generally, however, the court will reject this type of request.

9.9 Do I need to wait until the end of the divorce to get child support?

No. The court can enter an order of temporary child support shortly after the filing of the case. The procedure involves filing a motion with the court asking that the judge enter a temporary support order. Courts will require you to provide an affidavit summarizing your income and expenses as a companion to the filing. Often, however, people informally agree to a temporary support arrangement without going to court.

In temporary support hearings, judges do not always apply the guidelines. Bills and expenses need to be paid and the judge has to juggle all of the competing demands for limited finances. For example, the judge may order one parent to make the mortgage payment or pay other bills instead of child support. Family resources are strained during the divorce because of added family expenses, particularly when the two of you separate. Generally, judges look to both of your incomes and expenses and try to allocate the resources in a fair way.

Assuming the judge grants a temporary support order, the order will remain in place until the end of the case, or until the judge enters a different order. The amount of support in a temporary order does not always reflect the amount that will be paid at the end of the case. The judge will need to determine a fair amount of support at the end of the case, considering all of the circumstances, as they exist at that time.

9.10   Will I be taxed on my child support?

No. Child support is not considered income to the recipient and it is not a deduction to the parent paying it.

9.11   My spouse and I have agreed to a shared parenting schedule, with both of us having substantial time with the children. How will child support work under that arrangement?

If both parents have at least 146 overnights with the child, here is how support is calculated:

- The basic child support obligation is multiplied by 1.5 to calculate the shared child support obligation.

- The adjusted support figure is then allocated between the parents based upon their respective net incomes.

- Each parent's support obligation is computed by multiplying that parent's portion of the shared-care support obligation by the percentage of time the child spends with the other parent.

- The respective child support obligations are then offset, with the parent owing more paying the difference between the two amounts.

Here is an example of how a shared parenting schedule might impact support. Assume both parents have at least 146 overnights with the children and the baseline support is $3,000. That sum is adjusted to $4,500 ($3,000 x 1.5). Further assume that one parent has 70 percent of the combined net income and the other parent has 30 percent of the combined net income. The support obligation of the parent with the higher income is $3,150 (70 percent of $4,500) and the other parent's obligation is $1,350 (30 percent of $4,500). Next, assume that the parent with the lower income has 60 percent of the total time with the children and the parent with the higher income has 40 percent of the total time. The support obligation of the higher-income parent is calculated by determining 60 percent (lower-income parent's percentage of time) of the $3,150 support obligation, setting the total obligation at $1,890. The same is done for the other parent's obligation. The $1,350 obligation is multiplied by 40 percent (higher-income parent's percentage time), resulting in an adjusted obligation of $540. When the lower-income parent's obligation of $540 is deducted from the higher-income parent's obligation of $1,890, it results in a net obligation from one parent to the other in the amount of $1,350 per month.

9.12 Will my ex-spouse be required to contribute to any of the children's expenses, beyond the support that he or she is ordered to pay?

Yes, both parents will ordinarily have to share other financial responsibilities for the children in addition to the regular support payment. Both parents may be required to contribute to the children's health insurance and health-care costs, child-care costs, school fees, and extracurricular activity fees in addition to his or her regular support obligation. If the children have certain special needs, the court will consider having both parents contribute to those costs as well.

9.13 My ex-spouse is disabled, receiving Social Security disability. How does child support work under that circumstance?

You will receive dependent disability payments directly from the Social Security Administration. The sums you receive will be considered the child support and your ex-spouse will not have to contribute beyond those sums (unless he or she has other resources that would allow additional support).

9.14 My ex-spouse and I have agreed that each one of us will keep one child. My ex-spouse doesn't want to pay any child support but earns three times my income. What will the court likely do?

Where both parents have primary care of one of their children, the support each owes the other is calculated and the difference is then paid by the party owing more. The court still may deviate from this formula if appropriate.

9.15 How long does child support need to be paid?

Ordinarily, child support is paid until the child is eighteen years old. If the child has not graduated high school by his or her eighteenth birthday, support continues until the child graduates high school, but not later than his or her nineteenth birthday. Child support is not paid during college but either parent may seek contribution for the child's expenses both during college and while the child is at home on breaks. (*See* question 9.18.)

9.16 Does support automatically end when my child is eighteen or do I need to do something to end it?

Support does not end without a court order. Without a court order authorizing you to stop paying, you will continue to owe support, regardless of your child's age or emancipation. The support continues to accrue and your ex-spouse could collect those sums later. A few months before your child graduates (or turns eighteen, whichever is later) ask your lawyer to file a petition to terminate child support on the appropriate date.

9.17 My child is disabled: am I entitled to child support after he is eighteen?

If a child becomes disabled either before the divorce or during a period that the parents owe a duty of support, provisions can be made for the support of that child beyond his or her eighteenth birthday. The court can order that support be paid either from the income or assets of either parent. The court can also order that support be paid from the estate of a deceased parent. The support can either be paid to one of the parents, paid to a trust created for the benefit of the child, or paid to an irrevocable special-needs trust created for the child. When determining support for a disabled child, the court is to consider:

- The present and future financial resources of the parents, including their respective ability to save for retirement

- The standard of living the child would have enjoyed had the marriage not dissolved, along with any other equitable factors

- Resources of the child including any financial or governmental or other social service resources

9.18 Will my ex-spouse need to contribute to our children's college expenses?

A judge can order either of you to contribute toward your children's college expenses, assuming you both have an ability to pay. The judge will ordinarily not address the issue of college expenses at the time of the divorce unless a child is in college or will be attending college shortly. If the children are deemed too young, the judge will sometimes specifically reserve the issue for later determination. At the time that the children do attend college, either party can seek a contribution from the other. Even without a specific reservation, either of you could come back to court later, seeking an order requiring the other parent to contribute.

Judges consider a number of factors in allocating responsibility for college expenses. Here are some of them:

- The present and future financial resources of both parties to meet their needs, including, but not limited to, savings for retirement

- The standard of living the child would have enjoyed had the marriage not been dissolved

- The financial resources of the child

- The child's academic performance

In addition to tuition, the court may order the other parent to contribute to other costs: room and board, books and other supplies, fraternity or sorority costs, spending money, and other incidentals. Judges often use a formula when the parents' incomes are roughly equal: each parent pays one-third and the child pays the final one-third. The child's contribution may include grants or scholarships they obtain. There are no absolute formulas here, and the court employs a balancing test to come up with a fair result. However, there are certain conditions for ordering payments for college expenses.

In order to be eligible for educational expenses a child must maintain a "C" grade point average. Eligibility ends after the child receives his or her baccalaureate degree or marries. The child's enlistment in the military, incarceration, or pregnancy does not automatically exclude the child from eligibility. As another condition, the child must sign a consent allowing access to transcripts, records, and grade reports. The child's refusal to execute such a consent can terminate the parents' obligation to contribute.

Costs are based upon the cost of attending the University of Illinois in Urbana-Champaign. For example, the court will determine how much it costs for a child to attend school there and make that the cap of all expenses either parent must contribute. Regardless of whether the student lives on or off campus, costs are based on double-occupancy room for a University-sponsored residence (dormitory) and meal plan for the University of Illinois. The court can waive that cap upon good cause, however.

Parents may also be obligated to pay for medical expenses and medical insurance both during the school year and during periods of recess. Additionally, parents can be ordered to contribute for the expenses one of the parents incurs while the child lives at that parent's home.

The court can require both parents to cooperate in completing the *Free Application for Federal Student Aid (FAFSA)* forms and the court can allocate costs of college application fees and college preparatory classes. The court can order a parent to contribute for up to five college applications, two standardized college entrance exams, and one standardized college preparation course.

9.19 My ex-spouse is a procrastinator and poor money manager. Can the child support be taken from his or her wages?

Yes. Illinois law requires that child support be withheld from the paying parent's income unless extraordinary circumstances exist. Today, employers routinely withhold child support from employee wages just as they withhold taxes or retirement. Withholding is mandatory and not negotiable. From the paying parent's perspective, this is one less thing he or she needs to worry about. Plus, there are no questions about the payment being made and the responsibility for accounting shifts to the employer and the State Disbursement Unit. There are many advantages to both the paying parent and the support recipient by using the withholding system.

After support payments are withheld, they are sent to the Illinois State Disbursement Unit by the employer, which processes the payments and sends them to the recipient within forty-eight hours. You can also arrange to have the payments directly deposited into your account. Visit (www.ilsdu.com/index.jsp) for more information on the services offered by the Illinois State Disbursement Unit.

9.20 If my ex-spouse has income other than from an employer, is it still possible to get a court order to withhold my child support from his or her income?

Yes. Child support can be automatically withheld from many sources of income. These include unemployment payments, worker's compensation, and retirement plans.

9.21 My ex-spouse is friendly with his employer. I am worried that they will play games with the support withholding. Is that possible?

Anything is possible, but it is highly unlikely. There are severe penalties for an employer's failure to honor support-withholding orders. The penalty for the failure of the employer to timely turn over the support is $100 per day. Few employers are good enough friends to take on that obligation.

9.22 My former spouse is a self-employed contractor. Will the withholding order be effective?

In some situations withholding orders simply don't work. This is a good example. Consider creative approaches to ensure regular payments. Ask the judge to enter an order requiring an automatic transfer from your former spouse's account. If he or she has a history of irregular payments, ask the judge to require a bond, which is a large advance payment that is credited weekly for the support due. For example, the judge could order your ex-spouse to sell some property and place the proceeds with you to use for support for a set period of time. In appropriate cases, the judge may create a child support trust with your spouse's share of the property settlement. For example, if your spouse has demonstrated an unwillingness to pay support and is entitled to $50,000 from the divorce settlement, the judge can withhold that money and use it to pay the child support. Ask your lawyer about your various options.

9.23 The person I am divorcing is not the biological parent of my child. Can I still collect child support from my spouse?

No. Under Illinois law, only a biological or adoptive parent is obligated to pay child support.

9.24 After the divorce, if I choose to live with my new partner rather than marry, can I still collect child support?

Yes. Although spousal support (maintenance) may end if you live with your partner, child support does not terminate for this reason.

9.25 Can I expect to continue to receive child support if I remarry?

Yes. Your child support will continue even if you remarry. However, a remarriage would terminate maintenance.

9.26 What can I do if my former spouse refuses to pay child support?

If your former spouse is not paying child support, you may take action to enforce the court order with the help of your lawyer or Illinois court administrative services. If you choose to hire a private attorney to collect the support, that attorney would file the appropriate pleadings with the court to enforce the order. Commonly, if your spouse does not comply with a support order (or any other court order for that matter) your lawyer files a petition to hold your spouse in contempt of court. This proceeding is known as a *petition for order to show cause.*

Under this procedure the court conducts a hearing to determine if your ex-spouse is willfully ignoring the order or has some good reason why they haven't paid (for example, he or she lost a job). If the judge determines that the failure to pay is due to a legitimate reason, the judge will temporarily excuse the support payer. But even if your spouse doesn't have the money to pay, he or she is not excused from honoring the support order; the support continues to accrue until the judge enters an order modifying the obligation. The judge might require your spouse to look for work and report back periodically concerning his or her progress in finding a job, or the judge might require your spouse to sell property to pay back amounts due.

If, on the other hand, the judge finds that the failure to pay was willful or without good cause, the court will enter orders ensuring compliance. For example, the judge may order the sheriff to immediately take custody of your spouse and order him or her incarcerated until a portion or all of the back amounts due (known as the *arrearage*) are paid. Or the judge may give your spouse two weeks to pay the arrearage and if it's not paid, your spouse must turn himself or herself into the county jail to serve time until a predetermined amount is paid. If he or she flees, a warrant will be issued for his or her arrest and the person will become a fugitive.

Also, if the judge determines that the failure to pay support was "without substantial cause or justification," the judge will order your spouse to reimburse you the attorney's fees and costs you incur collecting the support. This provision is mandatory; the judge must order that the fees be reimbursed.

A child support arrearage is considered a judgment, and under Illinois law it accrues simple interest at the rate of 9 percent per annum. If your spouse owes you $5,000, for example, you are entitled to interest at the rate of $450 per year or $37.50 per month. Like other judgments, you can independently collect the amount due through garnishments, turnover order (levies against property), or other collection efforts.

If you prefer to use free state resources, you must contact your local office of the Illinois Department of Healthcare and Family Services (HFS) or (www.illinois.gov/hfs/ChildSupport/parents/Pages/Apply.aspx). This agency is responsible for child support collection. Assuming you are eligible for assistance, the matter will be referred to your local state's attorney office or the attorney general's office for support-enforcement services. The state has significant power to use its resources to collect your support. For example, the state is authorized to use the following procedures to collect support:

- Request that child support debt be included in the owing parent's credit report
- Collect the past-due amounts owed through contractual agreements with private collection agencies
- Place a lien against any real estate or personal property owned by the parent in certain circumstances
- Place a lien on an account in a financial institution in certain circumstances
- Have the support withheld from a 401(k) or other defined contribution account
- Request suspension or revocation of an Illinois professional license, occupational certificate, or hunting or fishing license
- Request suspension or revocation of the parent's Illinois driver's license
- Request a denial or suspension of the parent's U.S. passport
- Require the parent to post a bond, security, or other guarantee of payment when the noncustodial parent is not subject to income withholding
- Intercept state and federal tax refund payments
- Request state or federal criminal prosecution for non-payment in certain circumstances
- List the name and photograph of the parent on the Illinois Department of Healthcare and Family Services (HFS) website.

The power of the state is broad and far reaching, and it has resources beyond what a private lawyer can do. When you are confronted with a nonpaying spouse, consult with HFS to determine the availability of their services.

For updates on topics in this chapter visit (www.peskindlaw.com/legal-updates).

10

Maintenance

Maintenance is also known as *alimony* or *spousal support*. Illinois law authorizes a court to order one spouse to provide support for the other during and/or after the divorce. Typically, courts award maintenance in longer marriages, helping an economically dependent spouse get back on his or her feet. The policy behind maintenance is to recognize that spouses often sacrifice professional opportunities to care for children or assume homemaker responsibilities that benefit the family. As a result, if the marriage ends, that spouse needs assistance, sometimes permanently, to maintain a comfortable standard of living.

If a court determines that maintenance is appropriate, the court is to use certain legislative guidelines (discussed below) unless the court determines that the guidelines are inappropriate. The guidelines set forth the amount and duration of the maintenance.

10.1 My former spouse wants this divorce. Why is he entitled to maintenance?

One of the most difficult things for many people to accept is the notion that Illinois courts disregard issues of conduct or behavior when deciding financial issues. Since 1977, when Illinois adopted the *Illinois Marriage and Dissolution of Marriage Act,* our law has disallowed considerations of behavior or conduct when deciding the question of maintenance. The fact that your former spouse is initiating the divorce is immaterial to the need for financial support. Although it seems unfair that your former spouse's decision to divorce imposes this obligation on you, the judge will not consider who wants the divorce in determining any financial issues.

10.2 Please explain the various types of maintenance under Illinois law.

Under the statute (750 ILCS 5/504) there are three categories of maintenance:

- Fixed-term maintenance
- Indefinite maintenance
- Reviewable maintenance

If the court grants maintenance for a *fixed term,* the court is to designate the period which this maintenance is to be paid. Maintenance is barred after the end of the period during which fixed-term maintenance is to be paid. Under an *indefinite award,* the maintenance is to continue until it is either modified or later terminated by returning to court. *Reviewable maintenance* is set for a term, with a review to occur regarding the propriety of continued maintenance or whether it should be adjusted or terminated.

10.3 What will the judge consider when determining whether I am entitled to maintenance?

The judge will consider all relevant facts, including the following factors that are set out in the maintenance statute, 750 ILCS 5/504:

- The income and property of each party, including marital property apportioned and nonmarital property assigned to the party seeking maintenance as well as all financial obligations imposed on the parties as a result of the dissolution of marriage
- The needs of each party
- The realistic present and future earning capacity of each party
- Any impairment of the present and future earning capacity of the party seeking maintenance due to that party devoting time to domestic duties or having for-

gone or delayed education, training, employment, or career opportunities due to the marriage

- Any impairment of the realistic present or future earning capacity of the party against whom maintenance is sought
- The time necessary to enable the party seeking maintenance to acquire appropriate education, training, and employment, and whether that party is able to support himself or herself through appropriate employment
- The effect of any parental responsibility arrangements and its effect on a party's ability to seek or maintain employment
- The standard of living established during the marriage
- The duration of the marriage
- The age, health, station, occupation, amount, and sources of income, vocational skills, employability, estate, liabilities, and the needs of each of the parties
- All sources of public and private income including, without limitation, disability and retirement income
- The tax consequences to each party
- Contributions and services by the party seeking maintenance to the education, training, career or career potential, or license of the other spouse
- Any valid agreement of the parties
- Any other factor that the court expressly finds to be just and equitable

The starting point is to determine whether you can support yourself to maintain your standard of living during the marriage. If your marital lifestyle was one of country clubs and foreign travel and your income only allows club sandwiches and travel to the park next door, you may be a candidate for maintenance. Discuss with your lawyer the likelihood of obtaining maintenance based upon your individual circumstances.

10.4 What information should I provide my lawyer if I want maintenance?

If your lawyer advises you that you may be a candidate for maintenance, be sure to provide complete facts about your situation, including:

- A history of the interruptions in your education or career for the benefit of your former spouse, including transfers or moves due to your spouse's employment

- A history of the interruptions in your education or career for raising children, including periods during which you worked part-time

- Your complete educational background, including the dates of your schooling or training and degrees earned

- Your contributions to your former spouse's education and career advancement

- Relocations due to your former spouse's career

- Your work history, including the names of your employers, the dates of your employment, your duties, your pay, and the reasons you left

- Any pensions or other benefits lost due to the interruption of your career for the benefit of the marriage

- Your health history, including any current diagnoses, treatments, limitations, and medications

- Your monthly living expenses, including anticipated future expenses such as health insurance

- A summary of your standard of living during the marriage (eating out, shopping, expensive cars)

- A complete list of the debts for you and your former spouse

- Income for you and your former spouse, including all sources

- Whether you entered into any prenuptial agreements, and, if so, provide a copy for your lawyer

Also include any other facts that might support your need for maintenance, such as other contributions you made to the marriage, upcoming medical treatment, or a lack of jobs in the field in which you were formerly employed.

No two maintenance cases are alike and they are very fact specific. The better the information you provide to your lawyer, the easier it will be for him or her to support your claim for maintenance.

10.5 My former spouse told me that because I had an affair during the marriage, I am not entitled to maintenance even though I cared for our children for many years. Is this true?

In the past, infidelity was a bar to maintenance, but that is no longer the law in Illinois. Your right to maintenance will be based upon many factors, but having an affair is not one of them. The court will not bar maintenance unless you have a new relationship that is so advanced that it is in the nature of a marriage (*See* question 10.13 on the impact of a continuing cohabitation on maintenance).

10.6 How is the amount and duration of alimony calculated for new maintenance awards?

Assuming maintenance is determined appropriate, Illinois uses guidelines to determine the amount and duration of the award. The formula is based upon the net income of both parties. For orders entered before January 1, 2019, a different guideline is used based upon the gross income of the parties. This change is to reflect the changes in tax law abolishing the deduction for maintenance for orders entered after December 31, 2018. Any maintenance orders entered before the January 1, 2019 will remain tax deductible and remain subject to the former guidelines based on gross income.

For all new maintenance orders entered after January 1, 2019 the guidelines provide that the maintenance amount is to be calculated by taking 33 1/3 percent of the payer's net annual income minus 25 percent of the payee's net annual income. The amount calculated as maintenance, however, when added to the net income of the recipient, shall not result in the recipient receiving an amount that is in excess of 40 percent of the combined net income of the parties. This last provision provides for a downward adjustment in the amount of the maintenance if it places the recipient with income in excess of 40 percent of the combined net income of the parties. This guideline only applies to families whose total gross income is less than $500,000 combined and the payer does not have a support or maintenance obligation to a prior spouse or child.

The court has the power to deviate from the guidelines if the judge determines their application would be inappropriate. If the judge rejects the guidelines, the judge is to determine both the amount and duration of maintenance based on the same factors he or she considers in determining the propriety of maintenance in the first place. (*See* the bulleted factors in question 10.3.)

Assuming the court uses the guidelines, the duration of the awards are based upon the length of the parties' marriage. The statute provides that the court is to set the duration of the maintenance by multiplying the length of the marriage at the time the case was filed by the following factors. For marriages: less than 5 years (.20); 5 years or more but less than 6 years (.24); 6 years or more but less than 7 years (.28); 7 years or more but less than 8 years (.32); 8 years or more but less than 9 years (.36); 9 years or more but less than 10 years (.40); 10 years or more but less than 11 years (.44); 11 years or more but less than 12 years (.48); 12 years or more but less than 13 years (.52); 13 years or more but less than 14 years (.56); 14 years or more but less than 15 years (.60); 15 years or more but less than 16 years (.64); 16 years or more but less than 17 years (.68); 17 years or more but less than 18 years (.72); 18 years or more but less than 19 years (.76); 19 years or more but less than 20 years (.80). For a marriage of 20 or more years, the court, in its discretion, shall order maintenance for a period equal to the length of the marriage or for an indefinite term.

In application here's how the duration calculation works: Assuming the parties were married for 15 years and 6 months, the statutory percentage (.64) is multiplied by the length of the marriage. 15 years and 6 months equals 186 months. 186 X .64 = 119.04 months of maintenance. So under this formula the maintenance would last 119.04 months or 9.92 years. The statute is confusing and you should consult with your attorney for further guidance on these obscure calculations.

10.7 How is net income determined for the purposes of maintenance?

Net income for the purposes of maintenance calculation is determined in the same way that net income is determined for determining child support (*See* question 9.4.)—that is, gross income from all sources minus properly calculated taxes.

10.8 I already have an existing maintenance order and want to modify it. How will the judge determine maintenance for orders entered before January 1, 2019?

First of all, in order to modify a prior maintenance order, you will need to show that there has been a substantial change in circumstances. If so, then the judge can adjust a prior maintenance order. Sometimes people negotiate agreements that limit their ability to modify maintenance orders. In that event, regardless of a subsequent change in circumstances, the original order will not be subject to a modification.

The law is currently in flux as to whether the court will apply the guidelines in existence at the time the original order entered or whether the court will determine the modified amount based upon other considerations. Consult with your lawyer to determine the likely result of a modification motion.

10.9 My former spouse makes a lot more money than reported on our tax return. How can I prove my former spouse's real income?

First of all, tax returns don't always tell the whole story about someone's income. For example, regular gifts received would not be reflected on the return. If your former spouse is self-employed, corporate distributions (distinguished from wages or dividends) would not necessarily show up on the personal return. Also, personal expenses paid by the family business will not always show up on the personal return. Finally, if your former spouse has access to cash that he or she doesn't declare, that may not be reflected on the return.

145

In these circumstances, your lawyer can take a number of actions to determine your spouse's income with greater accuracy. These include:

- Conduct more-thorough discovery, including review of W-2s, corporate tax returns, K-1 disclosures on stocks, and personal financial statements prepared for creditors.

- Examine check registers and bank deposits. If income deposited exceeds income disclosed, that is a way to prove more income.

- Conduct a lifestyle analysis, to prove that the cost of maintaining your lifestyle exceeds disclosed income.

- Take depositions of third parties who have knowledge of income or spending by your former spouse. For example, if you know someone paid your former spouse cash, your lawyer can subpoena that person to testify to that fact. If the money wasn't deposited into any accounts or reflected anywhere as income, that would help support your claim.

- Subpoena records of places where your former spouse has made large purchases or received income.

- Subpoena banks where your former spouse has received financing to obtain personal disclosures concerning your former spouse's income.

Lawyers often hire forensic accountants, who are trained to investigate these types of matters. The accountant will attempt to ascertain your former spouse's "real" income rather than the sums disclosed on the tax return. Also, lawyers sometimes hire experts to help you prepare a lifestyle analysis. A lifestyle analysis reconstructs your expenditures over a sample period of time. Assuming your paid family expenses exceed your former spouse's declared income, the analysis confirms the existence of other undisclosed income. Discuss your options with your lawyer.

10.10 What is the difference between *maintenance* and *property settlement*?

Maintenance and the division of property serve two distinct purposes, even though judges consider many of the same factors when deciding these two issues. The purpose of maintenance is to pay for your continued support, whereas the purpose of a property division is to distribute the marital assets fairly between you and your former spouse.

If you remarry or die, maintenance ends. In contrast, if money is still owed to someone from the property division at the time of his or her remaraige or death, the former spouse has a continuing duty to pay that money either to the remarried spouse or if dead, the estate or heirs. Unlike maintenance, a property settlement is not forgiven by virtue of your death.

10.11 Prior to getting married I foolishly entered into a prenuptial agreement that denies me any claims to maintenance. I hear prenuptial agreements are easy to break. Is this true?

No, this is not true. In fact, when prenuptial agreements are properly prepared and executed, courts enforce them. If the agreement limits or eliminates maintenance, and you can prove "undue hardship in light of circumstances not reasonably foreseeable at the time of the execution of the agreement," the judge can order maintenance despite the limitation in the agreement. The term *undue hardship* means that you will be destitute without the maintenance. Without that situation, the court will not grant you maintenance if you agreed to waive it in your prenuptial agreement. (*See* chapter 13 on prenuptial agreements.)

10.12 My lawyer expects my case to go on for at least a year: am I entitled to temporary maintenance during the case?

Yes, the law allows a party who needs assistance to seek temporary maintenance while the case is pending. The amount of the temporary maintenance has little bearing on the final amount because the judge considers different factors in determining the temporary amount. In a temporary order, for example, the judge may order your former spouse to pay certain bills and give you a smaller amount for your personal expenses. At the conclusion of the case, your expenses will be different and thus the amount will likely vary.

10.13 Does remarriage affect my maintenance?

Yes, the following four circumstances automatically end one's right to receive maintenance (unless there is a prior agreement otherwise):

- The recipient's remarriage
- The recipient cohabiting with another person on a continuing conjugal basis
- The death of the paying party
- The death of the receiving party

If a recipient remarries, the maintenance automatically terminates. People sometimes negotiate non-modifiable maintenance that continues despite their remarriage, but that is rare. The general rule is that maintenance terminates automatically upon the recipient's remarriage. If you remarry and don't tell your former spouse, it is possible that the court may make you pay back sums received after the remarriage. In contrast, the remarriage of the paying party does not affect the maintenance.

If the recipient enters into a serious relationship, that may also terminate maintenance. The legal standard is whether the new relationship is a "continuing conjugal relationship." This means that the new relationship is a committed relationship similar to a marriage. This rule also applies to same-sex relationships. If you live with your new partner, that generally ends maintenance.

Termination based upon cohabitation applies even during the divorce case. If you move in with your partner during the case, you become ineligible for maintenance both temporarily and at the end of the case. This remains true even if you break up with your partner before the end of the case. Once you cohabitate, your eligibility for maintenance from your former spouse ends forever.

Maintenance also ends if the paying party dies. It is important, when negotiating your agreement, to secure your maintenance with life insurance. Finally, maintenance ends when the maintenance recipient dies. The recipient's estate or heirs do not continue to receive maintenance unless a prior agreement permits the continued payment after death.

10.14 What can I do if my former spouse stops paying maintenance?

Like child support, maintenance payments can be withheld from the paying party's wages. Ask for such an order to secure your payment. If your former spouse owns real estate, the court can order that a lien be placed on his or her property to secure payment as well. The lien protects you if the payments aren't made and would require the sale of the property to pay you. Also, missed maintenance payments are considered a series of judgments and accrue simple interest at the rate of 9 percent annually.

Judges can enforce their orders, including maintenance orders. If your former spouse willfully violates a court order, the court can enforce the order by imprisonment if necessary. If you move from the county or state where the original order was entered, you may need to file the proceeding for enforcement in the county where the divorce judgment was entered. Consult with an attorney to determine where enforcement proceedings must occur.

10.15 My former spouse told me that he or she is going to file for bankruptcy to avoid paying me maintenance. Can he or she do this?

No. Maintenance payments are considered *domestic support obligations,* also known as *DSOs.* Under bankruptcy law, one cannot avoid paying a DSO by discharging it in bankruptcy. The maintenance continues regardless of a bankruptcy.

10.16 Can I return to court to modify maintenance?

Maintenance orders are usually modifiable if there has been a substantial change in circumstances since the last order. For example, if either party's income substantially increases, the court could modify the maintenance based upon those changed circumstances. Also, if either party's expenses substantially change, the court could modify the maintenance based upon that as well. In order to modify the order, you will need to file a motion to modify, alleging the specific change in circumstances.

The change in circumstances must have been unforeseen at the time of the entry of the last court order. For example, if a party knew that the other party was going to start working at a new job and earning more income when the original order was entered, he or she could not use that fact as a basis to later modify the order.

Some parties agree to make their maintenance orders non-modifiable, either as the amount of the payment or the duration of the payment. If you enter into an agreement making the maintenance non-modifiable either in whole or in part, the court will honor that agreement and disallow you the ability to modify the maintenance.

10.17 In my divorce, I waived maintenance. I have lost my job and need assistance. Can I go back to court and ask for maintenance?

Probably not. Once you waive maintenance, you waive it forever and the court will not allow you to come back later and seek assistance. Some divorce decrees reserve maintenance. This means that although no maintenance is initially paid, you have a right to come back to court later and ask for it. A reservation of maintenance is different from a waiver. Waivers are final and forever. Check with your lawyer or review your decree to see whether you waived or reserved maintenance. If waived, you are probably out of luck.

For updates on topics in this chapter visit (www.peskindlaw.com/legal-updates).

11

Property and Debt

There are three steps to resolving property issues in a divorce: classification, valuation, and distribution. When we classify property, we determine if it is marital or non-marital property. The property also needs to be valued; sometimes people agree on value and sometimes experts are used to value the property. Finally, the court needs to distribute the property. We will cover these topics in this chapter.

Resolution of property issues also involves the allocation of debt. What is the nature of the debt? Who incurred the debt and when? The judge has the responsibility to divide debt as well as property at the time of divorce. Issues of property and debt are considered together to determine a fair or equitable result for both parties. The court also considers maintenance in connection with dividing property. The amount of maintenance may affect the amount of property awarded and vice versa.

Distribution of property can be very involved and complicated. This process involves a substantial amount of work by your attorney. Lawyers need a higher level of expertise to handle complicated property issues. Make sure you consult an attorney whose skills are commensurate with the property issues involved in your case.

11.1 What system does Illinois use for dividing property and debt?
Illinois law uses the principles of *equitable distribution* to divide property and the debts. Under an equitable distribution

151

system, the court considers a number of factors to fairly divide the assets and debts. However, equitable doesn't always mean equal.

The court could decide to award one person more or less than half. Although a 50/50 division is usual, judges sometimes deviate from that percentage. One factor the court can't consider is fault or conduct. One party may have been a saint and the other a sinner, but it would have no bearing on the division of property.

11.2 Please explain the significance of marital versus non-marital property.

Property is classified in one of three ways: marital property, nonmarital property of one spouse, or nonmarital property of the other spouse. If the property is the nonmarital property of either spouse, it remains his or her property and is not subject to division in divorce. If, on the other hand, the property is considered marital property, it must be divided in the divorce.

Illinois divorce law generally does not consider title to property. In other words, if your husband buys a vehicle during the marriage and places it in his name alone, that fact does not mean the car is his nonmarital property. Rather, Illinois law considers how the vehicle was acquired: when, and with what money. The fact that he placed it only in his name has no bearing.

Only marital property is divided in a divorce case. Obviously a car cannot be cut in half. If the car is worth $10,000, the person keeping the car would need to pay his or her spouse their share of the car. Sometimes, instead of giving the person a cash payment to offset the car ($5,000 in this example), assets might be traded. Perhaps the parties have a grand piano worth $10,000. The other person might keep that as an offset for the car.

This example illustrates how lawyers cobble together a property settlement agreement. All of the martial assets and debts are listed and then divided up by offset or cash payment. This inventory of assets and debts is often referred to as a *marital balance sheet.* Much of the case is spent trying to come up with the values in order to equitably divide the assets.

Frequently, lawyers use a marital balance sheet to summarize all of the assets and liabilities and propose scenarios for their division. On the page 154 is a fictional example of a marital balance sheet.

11.3 What are the general rules used to determine if something is marital property?

All property acquired by either party during the marriage (regardless of title) is presumed to be marital property. If a party claims a particular piece of property is nonmarital, that party must prove that:

- The property was a gift.

- The property was inherited.

- The property was acquired through a "like kind exchange."

- The property was acquired by income generated from a nonmarital asset.

- The property derives from debt paid for with non-marital money.

- The property was acquired after a judgment for legal separation.

- A valid prenuptial or postnuptial agreement excluded the property.

Here are some examples of those categories:

Property acquired by gift is considered the nonmarital property of the person receiving the gift. For example, assume Bob bought Betty a $20,000 diamond ring as an anniversary present; if they later divorce, the ring is Betty's nonmarital property. Or if Bob's parents gave him an expensive watch for his birthday, the watch would be Bob's nonmarital property and Betty has no interest in it. This rule applies to cash gifts or any other gifts made to one of the parties either before or during the marriage.

If one of the parties inherits money or property during the marriage, the inheritance is also nonmarital property as long as it is not commingled with marital property or transferred to the other spouse. For example, assume Bob inherited $20,000 from his mother. If he kept that money in a separate account,

153

Marital Balance Sheet

Property	Marital Value	Spouse 1	Spouse 2
Real Property			
2280 Woodview Lake Rd. St. Charles, Illinois	$1,400,00.00		$1,400,00.00
Less: Chase Bank Mortgage #99990000999	$(280,000.00)		$(280,000.00)
Less: Standard Federal Bank line of credit #000999000	$(57,000.00)		$(57,000.00)
1225 Cottage Drive Rd, Chalesvoix, Michigan (50%)	$(100,000.00)	$(100,000.00)	
Accounts			
Chase Bank checking #112233344455	$15.000.00	$15,000.00	
Chase Bang savings #1122333444556	$35,000.00	$35,000.00	
Bank of America checking #999888777666	$5,000.00		$5,000.00
Merrill Lynch #999-6675	$105,000.00		$105,000.00
Legg Mason #10101010	$10,000.00	$10,000.00	
Smith Barney Citigroup #44449999	$40,000.00	$40,000.00	
Retirement Benefits/Accounts			
Johnson Company, Inc. 401(k)plan	$125,000.00	$62,500.00	$62,500.00
Standard Federal Bank IRA #000111555 (rollover)	$25,000.00	$12,500.00	$12,500.00
Chase Bank IRA #33532210	$25,000.00	$12,500.00	$12,500.00
Ford Motor Company Salaried Employees Pension Plan	QDRO	2/3 via QDRO	1/3 via QDRO
Business Interests			
Johnson Company, Inc. (50%)	$600,000.00	$600,000.00	
Hidden Valley Apartments, L.P. (2%)	$50,000.00	$50,000.00	
100 Acre Woods Apartments (3%)	—	—	
Gifts R Us (100%)	$5,000.00		$5,000.00
Life Insurance			
Northwestern Mutual policy #12125555	$85,000.00	$85,000.00	
Left Coast Insurance policy #99903333	—	—	
Other			
2004 Ford Windstar	$20,000.00		$20,000.00
Less: Ford Motor Credit loan #9990111	$(12,000.00)		$(12,000.00)
2006 Mercedes S500	—		
1966 Corvette	$25,000.00	$25,000.00	
TOTAL ASSETS	**$2,321,000.00**	**$1,047,500.00**	**$1,273,500.00**
UNSECURED LIABILITIES			
Credit Cards			
American Express #3000-0000-0000	$(1,000.00)	$(1,000.00)	—
U.S. Bank Visa #4000-0000-0000	—	—	—
Saks #99111008	$(14,000.00)	$(14,000.00)	—
Other			
Dr. Jones (marriage counselor)	$(3,000.00)	$(3,000.00)	—
Dr. Bradeu (children's psychologist)	$(2,000.00)	$(2,000.00)	—
TOTAL LIABILITIES	**$(20,000.00)**	**$(20,000.00)**	**—**
MARITAL NET WORTH	**$2,301,000.00**	**$1,027,500.00**	**$1,272,500.00**
Mortgage on Marital Home to Equalize		$170,500.00	$(170,500.00)

it would remain his property at the time of the divorce. If, on the other hand, he put it into a joint checking account, it probably becomes marital property. As another example, if Bob inherited a house and put Betty's name on the deed, that nonmarital inheritance would become marital property by Bob placing his wife's name on title to the property. Any time someone has nonmarital property, he or she may (sometimes inadvertently) convert it to marital property by mixing it with marital property or placing a spouse's name on the title.

Property exchanged for nonmarital property may also be considered nonmarital property. This is called a *like kind exchange*. Assume before the marriage Betty owned an apartment building located on Elm Street. After the marriage, she sold the Elm Street property and received $100,000. She then took that $100,000 and bought a new property on Oak Street. Assuming she didn't put Bob's name on the Oak Street property and used no martial funds, the Oak Street property would be considered her nonmarital property. This principle would apply to any new asset purchased with money from the sale of a nonmarital asset, as long as it is kept separate. If, instead of buying Oak Street, Betty invested the $100,000 in stocks in her name alone, those stocks would be considered her nonmarital property.

Also, income generated from nonmarital assets, which is kept separate, is nonmarital property. If Betty owned stock in a business before the marriage and received dividends, the dividends are her nonmarital property (assuming she didn't commingle them with marital money). Classification of property can be very complicated, particularly when one of the parties has an interest in a business. Make sure to consult with a qualified attorney if either you or your spouse has any business interests.

11.4 We used joint money to put a deck on my husband's nonmarital property: do I have any claim to that money?

Generally, if marital property is used to enhance one of the party's nonmarital property, you may be able to recoup a portion of the money. Assuming the money paid for the deck is traceable (it can be identified), and it was not a gift by you to your husband, the judge may have your husband reimburse you the money. The judge has the discretion to consider this fact in dividing other assets and is not required to give you a dollar-for-dollar reimbursement.

Assuming the judge permits a reimbursement, here is how it might work: if you paid $10,000 for the deck, your husband owes the marital estate $10,000. Assuming all the assets were split 50/50, he would owe you an extra $5,000 (one half of the $10,000 for the deck) at the time of the divorce. You would either be paid cash, or you might receive another asset as an offset. Alternatively, the judge might make him pay the money back in installments.

11.5 What factors does the judge look at in deciding how to divide marital property?

Property is ordinarily divided on a 50/50 basis, but under some circumstances the judge might consider dividing assets in other ratios. For example, the judge might give a homemaker 60 percent of the assets, to recognize the fact that his or her future financial circumstances are not be as promising as those of the working party. In general, here are the factors that a judge considers in deciding how to divide marital property:

- The economic contributions of both parties
- Contributions of services to the marriage: homemaker contributions, for example
- Dissipation of either party: actions taken to deplete the martial estate during a period when the marriage was undergoing an irreversible breakdown
- The length of the marriage
- The relevant economic circumstances of both parties
- Whether any prenuptial or postnuptial agreements address the distribution of property
- The age, health, station, occupation, amount and sources of income, vocational skills, employability, estate, liabilities, and needs of each of the parties
- The amount of maintenance paid or received

- The arrangements concerning parental responsibility of the children

- The future ability of the respective spouses to acquire assets or build wealth

- The tax consequences of the property division on each spouse

11.6 What is the date used to value the property?

Ordinarily, the judge values the property as of the date of a trial or as close to it as possible. However in appropriate circumstances, another date can be used either by agreement of the parties or if the judge feels it appropriate. The date a divorce is filed is immaterial to the question of the value of assets (although that date is important for the determination of the duration of maintenance). Therefore, if an investment was worth $20,000 at the time of filing, but went up to $25,000 at the time the assets are divided, you would use the $25,000 figure. The judge can, however consider the increase in value of assets that relate to a spouse's personal efforts during the divorce. If you are working out an agreement rather than going to a trial, you will need to agree on the value of the property as the basis of your property settlement agreement.

11.7 How does a judge determine who gets the house?

The first question is, who wants it? Often, neither party wants to keep the house after the divorce. In that event, you and your former spouse should determine when to sell the house, considering the needs of the children and the marketplace. Real estate can take several years to sell, and you and your former spouse will need to decide how to pay the mortgage, taxes, and repairs, pending the sale of the home.

If one person wants the house and the other doesn't, you need to determine the fair market value of the home by agreement or by an appraisal. Once the value is determined, you can determine its equity. The *equity* is the difference between the value of the home and the outstanding mortgages. The party keeping the house will need to pay the other spouse his or her share of the equity, typically 50 percent. That sum is either paid at the time of the divorce (if possible), at a future date, or by offsetting other assets.

157

Also, if one of you keeps the house, the other's name remains on the mortgage, regardless of ownership. For example, if you keep the house and your spouse gives you a deed transferring title to you alone, that transfer of ownership does not release your former spouse from responsibility for the mortgage. Your former spouse remains liable and if you miss a payment, it will affect your former spouse's credit. You may be required to refinance within a set term in order to release your former spouse from ongoing responsibility for the mortgage.

If both people want the house (and can afford it), the judge ordinarily permits the party with primary responsibility of the children to keep it. If there are no minor children, the judge might allow the parties to bid each other for the house.

In other words, if the husband is willing to pay the wife more than the wife is willing to pay the husband, he would keep it at that price and pay the wife, based up the amount he was willing to pay. There are no clear formulas for this dilemma, and judges will deal with this issue on a case-by-case basis.

11.8 I want to keep the house but am uncertain. What should I consider?

To help you decide whether you should keep the house, ask yourself these questions:

- What will be the impact on my children if the home is sold?

- Can I realistically afford to stay in the house after the divorce?

- After the divorce, will I be willing to give the house and yard the time, money, and physical energy required for its maintenance?

- Is it necessary for me to sell the house to pay a share of the equity to my former spouse, or are there other options?

- Would my life be easier if I were in a smaller or simpler home?

- What are my other housing options in my children's school district?

- Would I prefer to move closer to the support of friends and family?
- What is the state of the housing market in my community?
- What are the benefits of remaining in this house?
- Can I retain the existing mortgage or will I have to refinance?
- Will I have a higher or lower interest rate if I sell the house?
- Will I have the means to acquire another home?
- If I don't retain the home and my former spouse asks for it, what effect will this have on my parental responsibility in the case?
- Will my former spouse agree to the sale of the house now?
- How much will I likely have after the sale for a down payment on another home?
- What will be the real estate commission?
- What will be the costs (both time and economic) of preparing the house for sale?
- Will there be any capital gains taxes that I need to worry about?

Selling a home is more than just a legal or financial decision. Beware not to make this decision based upon the fear of change. People sometimes want to cling to their home as a life preserver in a turbulent time. Look at this issue realistically: if you will have to radically and unreasonably trim back your lifestyle to afford the house, it makes sense to sell it now and look at other more-affordable options.

11.9 My former spouse wants to keep the house and I don't object. What should I consider?

There are two factors that you need to consider: how your former spouse intends to pay you your share of the house equity, and the status of the existing mortgage. Does your former spouse have the ability to pay you now? Is he or she proposing paying you at a later date? Are you willing to accept an offset against the house (for example, taking more retirement money in exchange for the house)? Do you agree on the present value? If not, it will be difficult to determine a buyout amount. Even if you agree on the buyout amount, there may be other considerations. If your former spouse wants you to take less since he or she will have future realtor commissions, are you willing to discount your share? Usually judges don't allow offsets for future closing costs, including realtor commissions.

Assuming an agreement can be reached on the buyout amount and the terms of payment, the next question involves the status of the existing mortgage. If your name is not on the mortgage, there is nothing to worry about. But if your name is on the mortgage, you need to be concerned. You are not released from liability by simply giving up your interest to your former spouse, even if he or she agrees to pay and keep the mortgage current. You legally remain liable on the mortgage, and any missed or late payments would affect your credit, regardless of the terms of your divorce agreement. For this reason, you will want your former spouse to refinance the mortgage within a short period of time, to limit your liability.

11.10 Our house is under water. How will a divorce judge address this problem?

One of the continuing by-products of the 2008 economic meltdown is the dramatic reduction in real estate values. Some people find themselves with a mortgage that exceeds the value of the real estate. This problem limits many people's ability to both sell and refinance their home. Discuss your options with your lawyer. Consider seeking a short sale from your lender. Under a short sale, the mortgage company agrees to take less than the full amount of the mortgage and writes off the balance. There may be a tax liability for the write-off, however. Determine whether there will be any taxes due on the sums written off.

Some people are so far under water that they simply stop paying the mortgage and wait for the lender to foreclose. During that period they do not pay their mortgage and, if appropriate, discharge any money owed in a bankruptcy. This is a dramatic option but it is appropriate for people in a hopeless financial landslide.

Finally, some people put off selling or refinancing their home, hoping that the market will come back and allow for the value to catch up with the debt. In that instance, provisions will need to be made in the divorce agreement to divide the property at a future date.

11.11 My former spouse removed $20,000 from our savings account and claims the money was lost. Is there anything I can do about this?

Yes, the law has a remedy for this type of behavior. If either party spends money on an improper purchase during the period when the marriage is breaking down, the judge can reallocate the sums misspent. This concept is known as a *dissipation of marital assets.* If your former spouse can't account for the missing $20,000, the judge might have your spouse reimburse the marital estate $20,000 from another asset to offset the loss.

The law does not allow one to "lose" money without being held accountable. One must specifically account for his or her use of money during the divorce and during prior periods where the marriage is breaking down. A claim that the money was used for living expenses isn't good enough; he or she needs to account for the specific expenditures or they will be accountable for the loss. Frequently, people spend money on new relationships while the marriage is breaking down. The party spending the money may need to reimburse the other spouse one half of the sums illicitly spent.

This general principle extends not only to people who loot the finances, but also to people who passively cost the family. An example of this latter scenario might be the spouse who stops paying the mortgage, despite having adequate funds, causing a foreclosure of the home. The court can consider that fact when allocating the remaining property.

Illinois law does not permit a court to consider fault or behavior in determining the financial issues in divorce, but this is one area where the court can compensate the spouse who has been victimized by their spouse's bad behavior.

11.12 My former spouse and I own a dry cleaning business. Who gets the business in the divorce?

Dividing an ongoing business poses certain challenges in a divorce. If both parties are actively running the business, they must decide who will keep the business after the divorce. Some people agree to continue on as co-owners, but that is rare. Usually, one of the parties keeps the business and buys out the other party. If you and your former spouse can't agree on who keeps the business, the judge will decide, usually awarding the business to the party more involved with ongoing operations. Sometimes people agree to sell the business and divide the proceeds.

The party who keeps the business will need to pay the other party their share of the value of the business. This principle also applies to professional practices, such as a medical, dental, or law practice. When the ongoing business or practice is profitable and owns assets, lawyers often hire a business evaluator to value the business. A business evaluator will consider the level of profitability of the business, the value of its assets, and its overall economic circumstances. Generally, more-profitable businesses have a higher value. The business evaluator will render an opinion concerning the value of the business. Often, both parties hire their own business evaluators as expert witnesses. Trials are often necessary when both parties' experts disagree on value and they cannot meet somewhere in the middle. In that event the judge will listen to the testimony of both experts and determine the business value based upon the evidence presented.

Once the value of the business is determined, either by agreement or by the judge, arrangements need to be made to pay the non-owning spouse his or her share. Assume a business has a value of $1,000,000. If the owner has sufficient assets to pay off the spouse at the time of the divorce, the judge will usually order the spouse keeping the business to pay the other spouse his or her share at the time of the divorce ($500,000 in this example). If sufficient funds are not available, the judge may allow the business owner to pay the spouse in installments over a period of time. For example, the judge might make the owner spouse pay annual payments of $100,000, securing the debt with business assets to ensure payment.

11.13 How are pets divided in a divorce?

Pets are considered property despite our emotional relationship with them. The judge has the power to allocate ownership or responsibility for any companion pets that are considered marital property. This includes ordering a "shared custody" type of arrangement. The judge is to consider the well-being of the pet when doing so. Consult with your lawyer to determine an appropriate strategy for maintaining possession of your pet. The law currently does not make any provision for "puppy support" however.

11.14 Are pensions and 401(k) benefits divided in a divorce?

Yes. To the extent that a retirement benefit was earned during the marriage, it is considered marital property and divided in a divorce case. The various issues related to division of employment benefits will be addressed in chapter 12.

11.15 Are there other types of assets I should be aware of?

All of the following (assuming they are marital property) may be divided between the parties in a divorce case:

- Collections
- Art or antiques
- Boats or expensive recreational equipment
- Cars, motorcycles, trailers, and recreational vehicles
- Cash value of insurance policies
- Annuities
- IRAs and other private retirement funds
- Defined benefit or defined contribution plans
- Tools or equipment
- Furniture and furnishings
- Investments
- Stock, partnership, and, LLC interests
- Real estate
- Accounts receivable (loans to third parties that are owed back to either of you)

- Patents, trademarks, or other intellectual property
- Oil, gas, or other mineral rights
- Crops or livestock
- Stock options or futures contracts
- Leases that may be able to be capitalized
- Frequent-flier miles or other commercial rewards programs

If you or your former spouse has an interest in any of these items (or other items you may not be sure about), make sure you advise your lawyer, who can investigate whether you may be entitled to an offset or payment.

11.16 Who keeps all the household goods until the decree is signed?

The judge will ordinarily avoid deciding who keeps the household goods on a temporary basis. Most couples attempt to resolve these issues on their own rather than incur legal fees to dispute household goods.

11.17 My former spouse has a pending personal injury lawsuit. Is any portion of that money marital property?

Yes, personal injury or worker's compensation settlements or awards are considered marital property. Because a part of these settlements compensates the injured spouse for future lost income, judges often give the majority of the award to the injured spouse. If the injury or worker's compensation case is unresolved at the time of the divorce, the judge might predetermine each spouse's respective percentages and then require the party receiving the settlement to notify his or her former spouse when the case is resolved.

11.18 I put my former spouse through medical school working two jobs. Is his medical degree considered marital property?

No. In Illinois advanced degrees or professional licenses earned during the marriage are not marital property (or property at all for that matter). But the judge will consider your contributions when dividing the marital property. The judge may recognize your efforts by granting you more than 50 percent of the property. The judge will also consider your efforts when deciding the issue of maintenance.

11.19 My former spouse took out student loans during our marriage and expects me to pay half. Is this debt my responsibility?

All debts incurred during the marriage are considered marital debts regardless of which person incurred the debt. Technically, your former spouse's student loans are considered marital debt. Usually, however, judges allocate student loans to the person who obtained the education.

11.20 If I receive an inheritance, what do I do to protect it from becoming marital property?

First make sure that the money is not placed into a joint account. Don't combine the inheritance with other existing money. The best practice is to open a new account in your name alone and place the money in that new account. Don't place any other money into that account, unless it is additional inheritance or a gift. If you use any of the money to purchase anything, document the purchase and make sure the title to the purchased property is in your name alone. For example, if you buy a car with your inheritance, keep records showing the source of the funds used and make sure you place title to the car in your name alone.

11.21 I suspect my former spouse is hiding assets, but I can't prove it. How can I protect myself if I discover something hidden after the divorce?

Ask your lawyer to include language in your divorce decree to address your concern. Insist that your former spouse acknowledge that the agreement was based upon a full and complete disclosure of your former spouse's financial condition. Require your former spouse to complete written discovery vouching that all disclosures are complete. As an option, provide in your agreement that if undisclosed assets are discovered after the divorce, those hidden assets will be divided upon discovery.

11.22 My former spouse and I are farmers. What do I need to know about dividing our assets?

Farm operations can be complex because of the many sources of income and debts. Look for an attorney experienced in farm divorces and familiar with the *Federal Farm Bill* on federal funding for farmers.

These are the actions that might be needed in your case:

- Entering a temporary restraining order blocking the transfer of the farm assets

- Conducting more-in-depth discovery in order to gather information such as the timing of payments, contracts, agreements to withhold payment, prepurchased feed or fertilizer, and grain delivered but not receipted

- Hiring experts concerning farm economics

- Obtaining information under the *Freedom of Information Act (FOIA)* from federal agencies such as the Department of Agriculture or the Farm Credit Administration

- Using a forensic accountant to help investigate, including evaluating balance sheets and tracing cash flow

Work closely with your lawyer to be sure that you have a complete and accurate picture of your financial situation before entering settlement negotiations or proceeding to trial.

11.23 What, if anything, should I be doing with the credit card companies as we go through the divorce?

If possible, obtain individual and separate credit prior to the divorce. This will help you establish credit in your own name and help you with necessary purchases upon your separation. Begin by obtaining a copy of your credit report from at least two of the three nationwide consumer reporting companies: Experian, Equifax, or TransUnion. *The Fair Credit Reporting Act* entitles you to a free copy of your credit report from each of these three companies every twelve months.

To order your free annual report online, go to ⟨www.annualcreditreport.com⟩, call toll-free to (877) 322-8228, or complete an Annual Credit Report Request Form and mail it to: Annual Credit Report Request Service, P.O. Box 105281, Atlanta, Georgia 30348-5281. You can print the form from the Federal Trade Commission website at (www.ftc.gov/credit).

Your former spouse may have incurred debt using your name. Advise your attorney if this is the case. If you and your former spouse have joint credit card accounts, contact the credit card companies to close the accounts. Do the same if your former spouse is an authorized user on any of your accounts.

If you want to maintain credit with a company, ask to have a new account in your own name. Be sure to let your former spouse know if you close an account he or she has been using.

11.24 Will the judge consider debts when determining the division of the property?

Yes. The judge will consider the marital debts when dividing the property. For example, if you are awarded a car valued at $12,000, but you owe a $10,000 debt on the same vehicle, the court will take that debt into consideration in the overall division of the assets. Similarly, if one spouse agrees to pay substantial marital credit card debt, this obligation may also be considered in the final determination of the division of property.

If your former spouse incurred debts that you believe should be his or her sole responsibility, tell your attorney. Some debts may be treated separately from other debts incurred during the marriage. For example, if your former spouse incurred debt gambling, you may be able to argue that those debts should be the sole responsibility of that party.

11.25 My former spouse has filed for bankruptcy. How will this impact the divorce?

Bankruptcy affects a divorce in a number of ways. Once the bankruptcy is filed, the bankruptcy court will issue an *automatic stay* order, which instantly bars any creditors from collecting any debts, including any garnishments or lawsuits.

The stay applies to the divorce as well; the divorce court may not enter any orders affecting your former spouse's assets. If you are scheduled for a divorce trial, the bankruptcy stay may cause a continuance, since the trial judge can't enter any orders affecting your former spouse's individual assets or any assets that are owned jointly. The stay does not relieve your former spouse from the obligation to pay support or maintenance; nor does it block your ability to seek court orders setting support or maintenance.

If the bankruptcy is filed after the case is concluded, your former spouse cannot discharge his or her obligations to you. In other words, if your former spouse was ordered to pay you $100,000 as a property settlement, he or she cannot use the bankruptcy to avoid that obligation. Also, the bankruptcy will not affect your child support or maintenance orders. One cannot avoid support or maintenance by filing for bankruptcy. In fact, the bankruptcy may make it easier to collect your support because your former spouse will no longer have to pay other creditors.

Bankruptcy may pose a problem, however, if you have joint debts with your former spouse. If, for example, you have a joint credit card with a $20,000 balance and your former spouse files for bankruptcy, the credit card company can seek payment from you, regardless of any agreement requiring your former spouse to pay that bill. In this instance, it may force you to file bankruptcy as well, to avoid having your wages garnished for the debt. Although you may be able to seek reimbursement from your former spouse (regardless of his or her filing for bankruptcy), collecting the money involves a potentially expensive court proceeding.

Plan ahead. When negotiating your agreement, try to resolve any joint debts at the time of the divorce. For instance, if you have a joint credit card, and your former spouse agrees to pay for it, require that the card get paid off at the time of the divorce. Or have your former spouse roll the balance onto the new card in his or her name alone. Do a credit report on yourself and make sure there are no joint credit cards that you forgot about or that your former spouse took out without your knowledge. Make sure you cancel any joint cards or any other joint debts (a line of credit for example). At the very least, if it is impossible to get a joint debt paid off, have very clear language in the agreement that provides your former spouse will "indemnify and hold you harmless" from any responsibility. This special language will make it easier for you to collect money from your former spouse in the event that he or she files for bankruptcy and attempts to avoid the obligation. Also provide that if the credit card company sues you, your former spouse will reimburse you any fees and costs you incur defending the case or seeking reimbursement from that party.

11.26 My former spouse's business was valued at $1,000,000, but a year after the divorce, it was sold it for $10,000,000. What can I do?

That depends upon the circumstances. If your former spouse misrepresented or concealed certain important facts at the time of the divorce, you may have an opportunity to request a rehearing based upon fraud. However, if you agreed to the value of the business and didn't investigate its value prior to reaching the settlement, you may be out of luck. There is a good lesson here: make sure you do a full investigation concerning the value of all significant assets prior to entering into an agreement. Hire experts who have specialized insight into the value of certain hard-to-value assets. If you rely on your former spouse's disclosures about value, even if the disclosures are based upon incorrect information, you are stuck with the consequences unless there is proof of fraud.

11.27 What happens to the property distribution if one of us dies before the divorce proceedings are completed?

If your spouse dies prior to your divorce decree being entered, you will be considered married and treated as a surviving spouse under the law. Thus you would be entitled to any benefits allowed any other surviving spouse, including beneficiary of retirement benefits, life insurance benefits, and Social Security benefits.

For updates on topics in this chapter visit
(www.peskindlaw.com/legal-updates).

12

Benefits: Insurance, Retirement, and Pensions

Many people are confused about their rights regarding their spouse's benefits. There is a good reason for the confusion—this is a very complicated topic involving complex federal laws and Illinois divorce law. The federal laws that apply include the *Employee Retirement Income Security Act of 1974 (ERISA),* the *Consolidated Omnibus Budget Reconciliation Act of 1985 (COBRA),* and the *Social Security Act.* It is important to hire a lawyer who has experience in this difficult area of law to make sure your rights are protected.

Determining the nature and extent of employment benefits is challenging. Many times, the employees themselves are unaware of all their benefits. Therefore, it is vital that someone getting a divorce conducts a thorough investigation regarding all employee benefits before agreeing to a settlement. Profit-sharing plans, 401(k) benefits, pensions, stock options, and restricted stock units are just a few of the employee benefits that can be divided in a divorce case. Other benefits that must be considered include life insurance and health insurance benefits.

12.1 Will my children continue to have health coverage through my former spouse's work even though we're divorcing?

If your former spouse is currently providing health insurance coverage for the children, it is likely that he or she will be required to continue to maintain that coverage for the children indefinitely. The judge will allocate the cost of the benefit if there is a disagreement, but ordinarily the parent with the least amount of parenting time pays for the insurance in addition to his or her child support.

If both you and your former spouse have health insurance benefits for the children, the parent with the better policy will ordinarily be required to maintain the policy for the children after the divorce. Sometimes there may be advantages to both parents continuing coverage for the children and the costs and benefits of doing that will need to be explored.

12.2 Will I continue to have health insurance through my former spouse's work after the divorce?

Once the divorce is finalized, you are no longer considered a spouse. You are no longer eligible for health insurance coverage unless you pay for continued coverage.

Federal law requires your former spouse's employer to offer insurance to you for a period of thirty-six months after the divorce. Commonly known as the *COBRA* law, this federal law ensures continued coverage, subject to your paying for the coverage. Investigate the cost of continuing on your former spouse's employer-provided plan. Ordinarily, the cost for continued coverage is very high, and a private policy may be less expensive. And with *Patient Protection and Affordable Care Act,* passed in 2010, the advantages of COBRA coverage may become even less attractive.

If you are interested in accessing your rights to continued coverage under the COBRA law, you will need to make the election for coverage within sixty days from the entry of the divorce decree.

Begin early to investigate your options for your future health insurance. The cost of your health care is an important factor when pursuing maintenance and planning your post-divorce budget. For more information, consult the U.S. Department of Labor website (https://webapps.dol.gov/dolfaq/go-dol-faq.asp?faqid=247&faqsub=Consolidated+Omnibus+Budget+Reconciliation+Act+%28COBRA%29&faqtop=Laws+%26+Regulations&topicid=5&lookfor=COBRA).

12.3   What is a *QMCSO*?

A *qualified medical child support order (QMCSO)* enables a parent to obtain medical information for a child covered by his or her spouse's group insurance plan. The order requires the plan to communicate directly with the nonparticipant parent and avoids that parent having to work through the parent who has the coverage. Often, group insurers will only reimburse the plan member for out-of-pocket costs, regardless of who paid the cost. This can pose a problem if the parent who receives the reimbursement fails to voluntarily turn it over to the other parent. A QMCSO remedies this problem and requires a health insurance plan to reimburse whoever actually paid the child's medical expense. For more information, consult (www.dol.gov/agencies/ebsa/employers-and-advisers/guidance/information-letters/01-19-1995).

12.4   I know my former spouse has a *401(k) plan*. What exactly is that?

A *401(k) plan* is a type of retirement benefit offered by employers. Another similar employee benefit is a 403(b) plan. With these types of plans, known as *defined contribution plans,* the employee contributes a portion of his or her wages and the employer matches a portion of the employee's contribution. A defined contribution plan is an account in the employee's name, managed by the employer or a manager hired by the employer, for the benefit of the employees. The retirement account is invested and the employee receives periodic statements reflecting any gains or losses in the account. The account grows tax-free and over time the compounding effect can generate significant growth in the account. Also, defined contribution plans often allow the employee to borrow money against the plan and pay it back monthly.

Ordinarily, the employee may not withdraw the money before age 59½, without incurring a penalty of 10 percent. If there is a withdrawal, ordinary income taxes are due on the money removed in addition to the 10 percent penalty. Assuming the employee is over 59½ years old, the employee can draw money out without a penalty, needing only to pay tax on all money withdrawn from the account. If the employee leaves the employer, the plan can be rolled over into an IRA or another 401(k) plan with a new employer, without incurring taxes or penalties.

Generally, all contributions made during the marriage, plus any earnings or growth related to those contributions, are considered marital property and subject to division during a divorce. If your former spouse's employer "matched" that spouse's contributions, those contributions are also considered marital property. Any contributions made prior to the marriage (and any earnings related to those contributions) are the property of your former spouse.

12.5   How is a 401(k) account different from an IRA?

In many respects they are very similar. Both are accounts that cannot be accessed without penalties and tax until the owner reaches the age of 59½. Both accounts are taxed only when withdrawals are made. Both accounts can be inherited if the owner dies. They differ to the extent that a 401(k) is an employment benefit, and often managed by the employer or its representative. Ordinarily, an IRA is an "Individual Retirement Account," without employer participation. Both can be divided in a divorce.

A 401(k) is divided in a divorce by a *qualified domestic relations order (QDRO),* which is a court order directing the administrator of the retirement account to transfer an interest to an employee's former spouse. In contrast, one divides an IRA by either changing the name on the IRA, or directing the trustee or custodian of the account to transfer a portion into a new IRA account for the receiving party. If the money is transferred in this fashion, there is no tax liability to either party upon the transfer. After the transfer is completed, the party receiving his or her share shall own all funds in the IRA. If the receiving party then withdraws the funds, he or she is responsible for the taxes and penalties (if he or she is under age 59½). Make sure to consult with a lawyer or accountant before removing any money from these types of retirement accounts.

12.6   My former spouse often refers to her pension. What is the difference between a pension and a 401(k)?

We need to be careful with these definitions. Sometimes people generically refer to defined contribution plans as a *pension.* Traditionally though, a pension is different from a 401(k) or other defined contribution plans. Most commonly, a pension is a *defined benefit plan.* Unlike a defined contribution plan, a defined benefit plan pays the employee a monthly payment at some predetermined future date, usually after he or she retires. Normally, the plan pays the employee until he or she dies.

Some plans have a vesting period before the employee is eligible to receive pension benefits. In other words, if the vesting period for the pension is ten years and the employee leaves the company before the ten-years period, the employee would receive would receive no pension. Also, depending upon the terms of the plan, the pension may be forfeited if the employee dies. Sometimes, the employee may purchase survivor benefits for his or her spouse, which will be paid to the surviving spouse in the event of the employee's death. The surviving spouse's benefit is a separate annuity, which the employee pays for by reducing his or her benefit by the cost of that annuity.

Unlike the 401(k), a defined benefit pension has no investment account. The plan is a contract to pay a future monthly benefit, assuming all of the terms of eligibility are met.

With a *defined benefit pension,* if the employee is fired or leaves the employer, he or she cannot take the pension with them (although, if vested, the former employee will receive the monthly payment even after leaving the employer). Also, the benefit is not transferrable upon the employee's death. Finally, unlike many 401(k) plans, one cannot take a loan against a pension.

12.7 How do I determine my share of my former spouse's defined benefit pension?

Any retirement benefits earned during the marriage are marital property and subject to division. If your former spouse worked for a company for ten years during your marriage, you would be entitled to half of the benefits earned during the ten-year period. If your former spouse worked for that same company for five years prior to your marriage, you would have no claim to any of those premarital benefits.

In determining your share of the pension, courts often rely on a formula established in the case of *In Re Marriage of Hunt*, known as the *Hunt Formula*. Here is how it works: Think of a fraction. The denominator (below the line) is the total number of months your former spouse earned benefits. The numerator (above the line) is the total number of months your former spouse earned benefits while married. For example, if the employee spouse worked for a total of fifteen years (180 months) at the time of divorce and was married for ten years (120 months) during the employment term, the *Hunt Formula* as applied would look like this: 120/180, or reduced two-thirds. Thus, two-thirds of the total benefit is marital property and the nonemployee spouse would receive half of that sum or one-sixth of the total benefit. Any benefits earned after your divorce are not divided and remain your former spouse's separate property.

12.8 What is a *qualified domestic relations order* and how does it work?

A *qualified domestic relations order,* also known as a *QDRO,* is a court order that directs the administrator of a retirement plan to assign a portion of the retirement benefit to the nonemployee spouse at the time of divorce. Procedurally, the administrator must approve the QDRO before it is effective. Most of the time, the proposed QDRO is given to the plan administrator before the judge signs it. If the administrator rejects the order because it violates the terms of the retirement plan, the lawyer submitting the QDRO will need to modify it to satisfy the concerns of the administrator. Many large companies have forms or checklists the attorneys can use to ensure that the QDRO will be acceptable. Other companies don't provide any guidance and it may take many drafts to complete an acceptable QDRO. Because of the complicated nature of these matters, many attorneys sometimes refer QDROs to other lawyers who have more expertise in this complicated area of divorce law.

Once the order is approved and signed by the judge, the retirement account may be divided. If the retirement is a defined contribution plan (a 401(k) for example) the nonemployee spouse will be provided the following options:

- The nonemployee spouse may transfer the money into his or her own defined contribution account (if he or she has one with the employer).

- The nonemployee spouse may transfer the money into an IRA.

- The nonemployee spouse may take part or all out in cash (subject to paying any taxes).

If the money is rolled into a 401(k) or IRA, the transfer will not involve any tax; neither the spouse who receives the money nor the employee spouse will be taxed for the transfer.

If the retirement plan is a defined benefit plan (a pension), the administrator will recognize the order when the pension is eligible to be paid out. Sometimes, the nonemployee spouse has the right to start taking benefits when his or her spouse is eligible to start drawing, regardless of whether the spouse retires at that time and starts taking benefits. So if the working spouse was eligible to start drawing benefits at age sixty-two, and chooses to keep working, the nonemployee spouse may choose to start drawing the benefits then, regardless. The amount of the benefit may be adjusted, depending upon when it starts getting paid out.

Here is an example: Under a divorce decree, a husband was to receive 50 percent of his wife's pension benefit. The benefit paid out $2,000 per month when the wife turned sixty-two. The wife chose not to retire and start drawing the benefit, but the husband wanted to access his share. The administrator would send the husband a check for $1,000 per month for so long as his former wife was alive.

This is a simplistic description of a very complicated topic. Make sure you consult with a lawyer who has ample experience and knowledge in this area of law. A great resource can be found in a publication of the American Bar Association called *The Complete QDRO Handbook* by David Clayton Carrad.

12.9 My former spouse is in the military and has a military pension. Am I entitled to a share of that?

Possibly. Your entitlement to a share of your former spouse's military pension depends on how many years your former spouse served in the military and how many years you were married. To receive any benefits, your former spouse must have served for at least twenty years. Assuming he or she meets that threshold, you are entitled to a percentage of the military retirement earned during the marriage. You may not begin receiving your share of your former spouse's military retirement until he or she retires. If you have been married for at least ten years, you may receive your share directly from the government. Even though payments to a former spouse ordinarily end with the death of the service member, the service member spouse may purchase survivor benefits for a former spouse that pay benefits after his or her death. In order to receive those benefits, the elections for the survivor spouse's annuity must be made before the service member retires. The cost of that survivor benefit will need to be allocated as part of the divorce negotiations.

12.10 Are federal employee civil service retirement benefits subject to division in a divorce case?

Yes. Federal government employees are entitled to receive benefits either through the Federal Employees Retirement System or the Civil Service Retirement System. To the extent that they are earned during the marriage, these benefits are subject to division in a divorce. Unlike many private pensions, the ex-spouse is only eligible to receive benefits after the employee spouse retires. The benefits can be transferred directly from the government under a *court order acceptable for processing (COAP)*. This order acts like a QDRO, transferring to the former spouse his or her benefits directly. In the event survivor benefits are paid, those will end if the spouse receiving the COAP remarries before the age of fifty-five.

12.11 My former spouse is a firefighter. Am I still entitled to a share of his or her pension?

Yes. Under Illinois law, pensions of government employees are subject to division in a divorce case. Illinois has established a procedure to access these pensions, using a *qualified Illinois domestic relations order* also known as a *QILDRO*. These orders operate very similar to a QDRO. Under a QILDRO, the plan administrator is ordered to transfer a portion of the employee's retirement benefit to a divorced spouse. The order may also assign any death benefit (life insurance) for benefits earned during the marriage. There are no surviving spouse benefits, which means that if the employee spouse dies, the other spouse will receive no ongoing surviving spouse benefit (although certain death benefits may be available). These types of orders apply to employees receiving *Illinois Municipal Retirement Fund benefits (IMRF), Teachers' Retirement System benefits (TRS), State Universities Retirement System (SURS),* police pensions, and Chicago Public School pensions. There are a number of other pensions that these types of orders apply to and you will need to consult with your lawyer to determine their applicability to you or your former spouse's retirement benefit

12.12 My ex-spouse owes me $20,000 in child support and has a large 401(k). Can I collect my support from that?

Yes. A defined contribution plan, such as a 401(k), can be accessed to pay the back support, as well as the interest and attorney fees spent collecting the support. In order to collect the back support, a QDRO will need to be prepared and signed by your judge, directing the administrator to pay out the sums due. Also, because the account is being accessed to pay child support, your ex-spouse will be responsible for the taxes on the distribution. Although not all retirement plans can be accessed to collect back support, a defined contribution plan, with sufficient funds available, can be readily accessed to collect past amounts due.

12.13 My former spouse has stock options at work. Am I entitled to a share of those benefits?

Yes. Illinois law provides that stock options, whether vested or unvested, are marital property if the employer grants them during the marriage. A stock option is an employment benefit that allows an employee the right to purchase stock at a predetermined and usually discounted price. The court will allow the nonemployee spouse some interest regardless of whether the option is vested or eligible for payout. Because stock options are usually nontransferable, the court will either allow the nonemployee spouse to determine when to liquidate his or her share of the option or the court will allow the employee spouse to decide when to liquidate the option. Either way, the nonemployee would then be paid his or her share from the employee spouse directly. Because stock options are taxed to the employee as income when liquidated, any taxes due to the employee spouse are deducted before the nonemployee spouse is transferred his or her share of the option.

12.14 My former spouse frequently talks about her *RSUs*. What are they and do I have any interest in them?

An *RSU* is a *restricted stock unit.* A restricted stock unit is an employment benefit that bases its value upon the company stock, although stock is not actually issued at the time the benefit is first granted. Large companies commonly use this type of benefit for their top-level executives. The employee must fulfill a vesting requirement to receive his or her share. Depending upon the plan, vesting requirements are based upon the passage of time or by company or individual performance. After the employee satisfies the vesting requirement, the company distributes shares of company stock or the cash equivalent. If the recipient does not meet the vesting requirements, the units are forfeited back to the company. RSUs are treated like stock options in a divorce. The court will determine if the benefit was earned during the marriage and divide the marital share of the benefit.

12.15 My former spouse has a profit-sharing plan at work. Do I have a share of that benefit?

Yes. Any employment benefit that has any value and that was earned during the marriage is considered marital property and subject to division in a divorce case. Profit-sharing plans, employee savings plans, and any other unique employment benefit that has any value can be divided in some fashion in a divorce case. Some employees have "non-qualified" retirement benefits as well. These plans provide benefits when the employee leaves the company or retires. Since the plans are non-qualified, they are not eligible for division by a QDRO. Although any interest earned during the marriage is marital property, these plans are ordinarily divided at the time they pay out to the employee. Commonly, the nonemployee spouse's interest is determined at the time of the divorce, with provisions in the agreement that the employee spouse will pay the appropriate amount at a future date, when he or she receives the benefit.

12.16 I am not confident my former spouse knows all of her benefits. How can we make sure we determine everything that her employer offers?

It is not uncommon for people to be unaware of all of their employment benefits. If there is any uncertainty, it is good practice to issue a subpoena to the employer requesting the following information:

- The nature and extent of all benefits the employee spouse has an interest in. This includes insurance benefits (health and life), retirement benefits (pensions, defined contribution plans), and executive compensation (RSUs or non-qualified benefits).

- Any vesting schedules or conditions on the employee spouse's access to the benefits

- Any information about retirement benefits, including any literature about the plan and the summary plan statement

- Contact information for the appropriate person(s) to call or write with questions about the benefits. This would include any persons who administer the retirement plans.

12.17 I haven't worked outside the home during the marriage. Am I entitled to a share of my former spouse's Social Security benefits?

If you were married to your spouse for ten or more years, and you have not remarried, you may be eligible for benefits after you reach age sixty-two. For more information, consult the Social Security website at (www.ssa.gov). Generally, your marital benefits are roughly half of your former spouse's benefits (although your former spouse's benefits are not reduced to pay your share). You may have earned benefits before your marriage and you should determine if your personal benefits would be more than your marital share. Contact the local Social Security office in order to determine which is more advantageous.

Benefits: Insurance, Retirement, and Pensions

12.18 What orders might the court enter regarding life insurance?

If your former spouse has life insurance benefits at work, the judge can order him or her to continue to maintain the benefits, naming you or the children as beneficiaries for a period of time, to secure either child support or maintenance payments. Likewise, if a private policy exists, the judge can order a parent with a support obligation to pay the premium to secure child support or maintenance in the event of his or her death. Sometimes the judge may require the person receiving maintenance to pay the premium to secure his or her maintenance.

In general, judges have the coverage continue until the support-paying parent no longer has a duty to pay child support, college expenses, or, sometimes, maintenance to the former spouse. The amount of the life insurance is dependent on the support or maintenance being paid, and the lifestyle of the family.

For updates on topics in this chapter visit (www.peskindlaw.com/legal-updates).

13

Prenuptial and Postnuptial Agreements

Illinois law permits a couple contemplating marriage to enter into a contract known as a *prenuptial agreement*. This contract is sometimes called an *antenuptial agreement*. Historically, people sought these agreements for a second marriage, to preserve assets for children from their first marriage. Today, however, people often use these agreements for a first marriage to resolve issues if they later divorce. Assuming the agreement is properly prepared and executed, it is enforceable and difficult to break.

If your spouse-to-be approaches you about signing a prenuptial agreement, make sure you understand any rights you are giving up. Also, use the process to evaluate your intended spouse's character. If your future spouse is wealthy and insists on you waiving all of your legal rights to maintenance, property, and everything else for that matter, is this someone you really want to marry? Premarital agreements must be looked at cautiously because courts will enforce these agreements, regardless of future circumstances.

In contrast, a *postnuptial agreement* is an agreement that the parties execute after the marriage. Although postnuptial agreements are similar to prenuptial agreements, they differ in certain respects. Sometimes there are legitimate reasons to execute a postnuptial agreement, but manipulative people can use these agreements to plot a better divorce settlement. As with prenuptial agreements, make sure you consult with an attorney to understand your rights before signing any type of agreement.

13.1 What subjects can be covered by premarital agreement?

Parties may contract in a prenuptial agreement the following categories:

- The rights and obligations of each of the parties in any of the property of either or both of them whenever and wherever acquired or located

- The right to buy, sell, use, transfer, exchange, abandon, lease, consume, expend, assign, create a security interest in, mortgage, encumber, dispose of, or otherwise manage and control property

- The disposition of property upon separation, marital dissolution, death, or the occurrence or nonoccurrence of any other event

- The modification or elimination of spousal support (maintenance)

- The making of a will, trust, or other arrangement to carry out the provisions of the agreement

- The ownership rights in and disposition of the death benefit from a life insurance policy

- The choice of law governing the construction of the agreement

- Any other matter, including their personal rights and obligations, not in violation of public policy or a statute imposing a criminal penalty

Prenuptial agreements may not be used to predetermine child support. Also, people may not use a prenuptial agreement to bar his or her spouse from seeking attorney fees concerning child-related issues. Thus, a clause that provides that each party is to pay his or her own attorney fees in the event of divorce doesn't apply to fees spent in any contested parental responsibility or support issues.

13.2 I hear prenuptial agreements are easy to break. Is this true?

No. These agreements, if prepared correctly, are nearly impossible to break. Don't enter into a prenuptial agreement thinking it will be unenforceable if you divorce. Make sure you fully understand the implications of the agreement, as you will likely be bound by it.

13.3 My friend entered into a prenuptial agreement and waived her right to maintenance. She now has cancer and can't work. Will this provision be binding?

Not necessarily. The statute provides: If a provision of a premarital agreement modifies or eliminates spousal support and that…causes one party to the agreement undue hardship in light of circumstances not reasonably foreseeable at the time of the execution of the agreement, a court, notwithstanding the terms of the agreement, may require the other party to provide support to the extent necessary to avoid such hardship.

Assuming your friend's illness was not "reasonably foreseeable" at the time the agreement was prepared, the court may require her former spouse to pay maintenance to assist her.

13.4 My fiancé gave me an agreement to review and told me that his lawyer will answer any of my questions. Is this a good idea?

This is a terrible idea. Your fiancé's lawyer is concerned with your fiancé's interest, not yours. Even if you know and trust the lawyer, you should obtain your own independent lawyer so that you fully understand all of the implications of the agreement. These agreements significantly impact your financial future, and you shouldn't enter into the agreement lightly.

13.5 What exactly is the role of the attorney in a prenuptial agreement?

The lawyer's role varies depending upon the circumstances. If one of the parties initiates the agreement, that party's lawyer will usually draft the agreement along the lines that he or she wants, or based upon discussions between the parties. After the initiating party has approved the agreement, it is sent to the other person's attorney to review and evaluate. That attorney's job is to point out all of the consequences of executing the agreement. When someone is in love and eager to get married, he or she doesn't necessarily think about the "what if…" of divorce. The attorney must also discuss the implications of a party's death, as many agreements also address disposition of assets in the event of either's death.

It is not unusual for the attorneys to negotiate agreements over the span of several months. It is important that agreements be prepared well before the wedding to give everyone ample time to negotiate and prepare required financial disclosures. Finally, attorneys assist in the execution of the agreement, often meeting with both parties to make sure the agreement is properly executed and all final terms are satisfactory.

13.6 My fiancé asked me to sign a prenuptial agreement the day before our wedding. I know nothing about his finances and signed the agreement without speaking with a lawyer. Will this agreement be enforceable?

Maybe. Prenuptial agreements are enforceable unless the party challenging the agreement can prove he or she did not enter into the agreement voluntarily. The question of voluntariness depends upon a number of factors, including your receipt of a full financial disclosure from your fiancé and an opportunity to consult with an attorney. If you were not given a full disclosure, and didn't waive your right to a disclosure, you probably didn't enter into this agreement voluntarily. Don't ever sign an agreement without first consulting an attorney to determine its implications.

13.7 What other criteria makes a prenuptial agreement unenforceable?

Intent is at the heart of whether a prenuptial agreement is enforceable. If someone signed an agreement under duress, the agreement is not voluntary. Duress is defined by our Supreme Court as "a condition where one is induced by a wrongful act or threat of another to make a contract under circumstances which deprive him of the exercise of his free will." If someone can prove he or she entered into the agreement under duress, it is unenforceable. People have tried to claim duress based upon being presented an agreement on the eve of the wedding. That fact alone doesn't invalidate the agreement, despite its eleventh-hour presentation. It is thoughtless to present an agreement a few days before the wedding, but the other person always has the option to cancel the wedding. To prove duress, one must show more than bad taste, embarrassment, or annoyance.

Agreements considered unconscionable at the time they are executed are also unenforceable. As mentioned in an earlier chapter, an unconscionable agreement is one that is outrageous or oppressive. In order to evaluate the question of unconscionability, the judge considers the circumstances of the parties at the time the agreement was made. If the divorce judge determines that the agreement was unconscionable at the time it was made, it is not enforceable.

Also, agreements executed without full disclosure are invalid, although a party may waive his or her right to disclosure. If a party enters into a prenuptial agreement and waives the right to full disclosure, he or she cannot later argue the agreement is unconscionable based upon a lack of knowledge.

13.8 I waited to the last minute and didn't have time to do the prenuptial agreement. Can I do one after I get married?

An agreement executed after the marriage is called a *post-nuptial agreement.* The law permits these types of agreements, but the rules are different. Prenuptial agreements are guided by the terms of the *Illinois Uniform Premarital Agreement Act* and all of the rules discussed there. Postnuptial agreements are not covered and ordinary contract law applies. Thus, the postnuptial requires *consideration,* an exchange that is bargained for. If one party gives up something in the postnuptial, the other party must also give up something in return. If you ask your spouse to waive an interest in an asset, you will need to make a concession of some other sort as well. In contrast, a prenuptial agreement does not require consideration because the marriage itself is thought to be the "consideration" of the agreement. Also, unlike a premarital agreement, the postnuptial agreement can be challenged if it is totally unreasonable at the time of enforcement (rather than at the time of execution). Prenuptial agreements can only be challenged as unconscionable at the time it was executed.

As a practical matter, once you are married, your spouse has little incentive to agree to a postnuptial agreement. If he or she agrees to do so, your spouse should be given the opportunity to consult with an attorney to understand the implications of the agreement.

For updates on topics in this chapter visit (www.peskindlaw.com/legal-updates).

14

Taxes

There are always two layers to any divorce agreement. The first layer is the specific terms of the agreement—the property distribution, maintenance, and support obligation. The second layer is the tax implications of the agreement. It's not what you get that is important—it's what you keep after your tax liability is assessed. Find a lawyer who understands divorce taxation to help you structure a settlement that doesn't leave you with a surprise at tax time. When in doubt, have a *certified public accountant (CPA)* review your agreement and make sure there are no unanticipated tax consequences.

Tax law scares many people but the rules are generally straightforward. A great resource for this subject is Internal Revenue Service publication 504, which can be found at (www.irs.gov/pub/irs-pdf/p504.pdf). This IRS publication explains all of the tax rules applicable to divorces or separated persons.

14.1 Will either my former spouse or I have to pay income tax when we transfer property to one another under our divorce decree?

No. However, it is important that you understand the future tax consequences of a subsequent withdrawal, sale, or transfer after you receive them. If you are awarded a particular asset under your divorce agreement or judgment, you will be responsible for any tax when that asset is sold in the future. When negotiating, you need to consider this. Future capital gains tax on the sale of property should be discussed with your attorney during the negotiation and trial preparation stages of your case. This is especially important if the sale of the property is imminent. Failure to do so may result in an unfair outcome.

For example, suppose you agree that your former spouse will be awarded the proceeds from the sale of your home valued at $200,000, and you will take the stock portfolio also valued at $200,000. If you decide to sell the stock after the divorce, you may owe taxes. Assume you learn that its original price was $120,000 and that there is a gain of $80,000. You must pay capital gains tax on the $80,000 gain, leaving you a net sum of $188,000. Meanwhile, your former spouse receives the proceeds from the marital home worth $200,000, but pays no capital gains tax.

The point of this example is to illustrate that what you get is not always what you keep. Make sure you fully understand the short- and long-term tax implications of any agreement.

14.2 Is the amount of child support I pay tax deductible?

No. Child support is not tax deductible by the paying parent nor is it income to the parent receiving the support.

14.3 Is the amount of maintenance I am ordered to pay tax deductible?

If the maintenance is paid under a court order entered prior to January 1, 2018, the maintenance will be tax deductible to the payer and deductible by the recipient for so long as it is paid. If the order was entered after January 1, 2019, any deductibility will be denied. Thus for all post–January 1, 2019 orders the payer may not deduct the payment and the recipient will not need to pay tax in the maintenance as income.

14.4 During the divorce proceedings, is our tax-filing status affected?

The date you file for a divorce is unimportant; what's important is the marital status as of December 31 of the tax year. If your case is still pending as of that date, you are considered married and can file as married filing joint taxes, which usually benefits both parties because of a lower tax rate. As another option, you can file married but filing separately, in which case you each file your own separate return. By doing this, however, you both should expect to pay higher taxes. In the year the divorce is finalized, you will either file as single or head of household.

Tax planning is important. If your employer is withholding taxes at work based upon the "married filing joint" withholding status and you divorce, you may not have withheld enough for your new single filing status. Try to figure out how short you will be and adjust your withholding to make up the shortfall. Many people who conclude their divorce late in the year hold off finalizing it until January. By doing so, they remain eligible for the advantageous joint filing status for the previous year.

14.5 Am I in trouble if I filed joint returns and my former spouse did not disclose all income?

If you were aware that your former spouse had undisclosed income and signed the joint returns, you are equally liable for the consequences. Those consequences may include large penalties and possibly criminal sanctions for tax evasion. If, on the other hand, you signed the joint return and were unaware of your former spouse's undeclared income, you may qualify as an "innocent spouse" and avoid liability. Discuss your options with your attorney, including hiring a tax lawyer or amending earlier returns to reveal the undisclosed income.

14.6 Should I file a joint income tax return with my former spouse while our divorce is pending?

Consult your tax advisor to determine the risks and benefits of filing a joint return with your former spouse. Compare this with the consequences of filing your tax return separately. Often, the overall tax liability will be less with the filing of a joint return, but other factors are important to consider.

When deciding whether to file a joint return with your former spouse, consider any concerns you have about the accuracy and truthfulness of the information on the tax return. If you have any doubts, consult both your attorney and your tax advisor before agreeing to sign a joint tax return with your former spouse. If you do file jointly, you expose yourself to liability for any tax, penalties, and interest due to improper deductions or income not properly disclosed. Although the IRS may relieve you of responsibility if you are considered an "innocent spouse," it's better to avoid the problem by filing separately. A judge may order some people to file jointly, but if the judge knows about the possible problems, it is unlikely he or she will compel you to file jointly with your former spouse.

Prior to filing a tax return, try to reach agreement about how any tax owed or refund expected will be shared. Ask your lawyer to assist you in getting this in writing.

14.7 What tax consequences should I consider regarding the sale of our home?

When your home is sold, whether during your divorce or after, the sale may be subject to a capital gains tax. If your home was your primary residence and you lived in the home for two of the preceding five years, you may be eligible to exclude up to $250,000 of the gain on the sale of your home. If both you and your former spouse meet the ownership and residence tests, you may be eligible to exclude up to $500,000 of the gain. In today's economic climate, few people are confronted with a gain in excess of $250,000 and thus no tax is due on the sale proceeds.

If you anticipate the gain on the sale of your residence to be over $250,000, talk with your attorney early in the divorce process about a plan to minimize the tax liability. For more information, *see* IRS Publication 523, "Selling Your Home," or visit the IRS website (www.irs.gov) and talk with your tax advisor.

14.8 Who gets to claim the children as dependents?

The deduction for children in divorce is usually an issue resolved in negotiation and oftentimes is alternated between the parents. Although the child dependency exemption was eliminated starting in 2019, claiming the children postdivorce will still be relevant to determine who claims them for the child tax credit, which is directly related to who claims them on the tax return. Going forward, the credit is $2,000 per eligible dependent. Single filers with an income up to $200,000 and married filers with an income up to $400,000 will qualify for this benefit. This is up from the previous limitations of $75,000 for single and $110,000 for married filers.

14.9   My decree says I have to sign IRS Form 8332 so my former spouse can claim our child. Should I sign it once for all future years?

No. Child support can be modified in the future. If there is a future modification of parenting time or support, the parent entitled to claim the exemption could change. The best practice is to provide your former spouse a timely copy of Form 8332 signed by you for the appropriate tax year only.

14.10   Can my former spouse and I split the child-care tax credit?

Only the custodial parent is allowed to claim the credit. Since Illinois no longer recognizes the word "custody," the parent with the majority of time with the children is eligible.

If you not the primary parent and paying child care, talk to your lawyer about how to address this issue in your divorce decree.

14.11   Is the cost of getting a divorce, including my attorney fees, tax deductible under any circumstances?

Your legal fees for getting a divorce are not deductible. However, a portion of your attorney fees may be deductible if they are for:

- The collection of sums included in your gross income, such as maintenance or interest income

- Advice regarding the determination of taxes or taxes due

Attorney fees are "miscellaneous" deductions for individuals and are consequently limited to 2 percent of your adjusted gross income. More details can be found in IRS Publication 529, Miscellaneous Deductions.

You may also be able to deduct fees you pay to appraisers or accountants who help. Talk to your lawyer or tax advisor about whether any portion of your attorney fees or other expenses from your divorce is deductible.

14.12 Do I have to complete a new Form W-4 for my employer because of my divorce?

Completing a new Form W-4, Employee's Withholding Certificate, will help you to claim the proper withholding allowances based upon your marital status and exemptions. Also, if you are receiving alimony, you may need to make quarterly estimated tax payments. Consult with your tax advisor to ensure you are making the most preferable tax planning decision.

14.13 What is *innocent spouse relief* and how can it help me?

Innocent spouse relief refers to a method of obtaining relief from the Internal Revenue Service for taxes owed as a result of a joint income tax return filed during your marriage. If you file a joint return, and your spouse made misrepresentations regarding his or her income, the innocent spouse protection may relieve you from responsibility. Numerous factors affect your eligibility for innocent spouse tax relief, including:

- You would suffer a financial hardship if you were required to pay the tax.

- You did not significantly benefit from the unpaid taxes.

- Your suffered abuse during your marriage.

- You thought your spouse would pay the taxes on the original return.

Talk with your attorney or your tax advisor if you are concerned about liability for taxes arising from joint tax returns filed during the marriage. You may benefit from a referral to an attorney who specializes in tax law.

For updates on topics in this chapter visit (www.peskindlaw.com/legal-updates).

15

Going to Court

For many people, their perception of court is based on movies and television. We see the witness breaking down in tears after a grueling cross-examination. We see lawyers moving around the courtroom, waving their arms as they plead their case to the jury.

Hollywood drama, however, is a far cry from reality. Going to court for your divorce can mean many things, ranging from sitting in a hallway while waiting for the lawyers and judges to conclude a conference, to being on the witness stand giving mundane answers to questions about your monthly living expenses.

Regardless of the nature of your court proceeding, going to court causes most people anxiety. Perhaps your divorce might be the first time in your life that you have even been in a courtroom. Feelings of nervousness and uncertainty are normal.

Understanding what will occur in court and being well prepared for any court hearings will relieve much of your stress. Knowing the order of events, the role of the people in the courtroom, proper courtroom etiquette, and what is expected of you will make the entire experience easier.

Your lawyer will be with you at all times to support you any time you go to court. Remember, every court appearance moves you one step closer to completing your divorce so that you can move forward with your life.

15.1 What do I need to know about appearing in court and court dates in general?

Although some court dates are routine status hearings, which require the attorneys to appear and update the judge regarding case progress, other court dates will be more significant. As soon as you receive a notice from your lawyer about a court date, confirm whether you must attend and plan accordingly. Depending upon the level of communication from your lawyer, you may want to touch base a day before to confirm that the court date is still proceeding.

Ask your lawyer about the nature of the hearing, including whether you will be required to testify or whether the lawyers will simply argue the matter. Ask your lawyer if you should meet before the court appearance to prepare or take any other action in anticipation of the hearing. Often, lawyers may need evidence; ask the lawyer if there is anything you should provide in advance or bring to the hearing. Find out how long the hearing is expected to last. It may be as short as a few minutes or as long as a day or more.

If you plan to attend the hearing, determine where and when to meet your attorney. Depending upon the type of hearing, your lawyer may want you to arrive in advance of the scheduled hearing time to prepare.

Make sure you know the location of the courthouse, where to park, and the floor and room number of the courtroom. Planning for such simple matters can eliminate unnecessary stress. If you want someone to go to court with you to provide you support, check with your attorney first.

15.2 When and how often will I need to go to court?

Whether and how often you will need to go to court depends upon a number of factors. Depending upon the complexity of your case, you may have only one hearing. In highly contested cases, you may be attending court several times per month. This is another good reason to try to maintain civility with your former spouse.

There are two types of hearings: *substantive hearings* and *procedural hearings*. Attorneys typically appear alone at procedural hearings. These include requests for the other side to provide information or for the setting of certain deadlines.

These hearings are often brief and frequently held in the judge's office, referred to as *chambers,* rather than in the courtroom. Both parties and their attorneys ordinarily attend substantive hearings, which may include negotiating temporary parenting issues or support hearings. Your attorney may tell you that you need not appear; however many people like to go to court to follow the progress of the case. Make sure to tell your attorney in advance if you intend to appear.

If you and your spouse settle all of the issues in your case, a final hearing will be held. This hearing is called a *prove-up.* If your case proceeds to trial, your appearance will be required for the duration of the trial. In Illinois, divorce matters are heard before a judge only; juries do not hear divorces.

15.3 How much notice will I receive about appearing in court?

The amount of notice you will receive for any court hearing can vary from several weeks to a few days. If something is considered an emergency, the notice may even be sooner.

15.4 I am afraid to be alone in the same room with my spouse. How can I avoid this when I go to court?

Talk to your lawyer about your concerns. Prior to any court hearing, you and your spouse may be asked to wait while your attorneys meet with the judge to discuss preliminary matters. If your case is the only case scheduled, there will not be other people in the courtroom. If being alone with your spouse is a concern, there are precautions you can take. For example, you might ask that you or your spouse wait in different locations. Or, take a friend or family member with you. You can also ask your attorney to advise court security or a bailiff of your concerns, and ask them to keep an eye on you.

15.5 Do I have to go to court every time there is a court hearing on any motion?

Not necessarily. The judge will decide some matters after listening to the arguments by the lawyers. Sometimes these hearings are conducted in the courtroom. At other times they are held in the judge's chambers. Typically, when matters are taken to the judge's chambers, the divorcing parties are not present.

If you would like to be present for the argument, ask your attorney if the argument can be conducted in the courtroom rather than in chambers. There may be reasons your lawyer wants to argue the matter in chambers and you should discuss that with your attorney. Although you undoubtedly are interested in all aspects of the case, if your lawyer feels that he or she can more effectively argue the matter in chambers, you should defer to that judgment.

15.6 My spouse's lawyer keeps asking for *continuances* of court dates. Is there anything I can do to stop this?

Continuances are postponed court dates and are all too common in divorces. A court date might be postponed for many reasons, including scheduling conflicts or the lack of availability of one of the parties or an important witness. Sometimes cases are continued because attorneys are not prepared.

Discuss with your attorney your desire to move your case forward without further delay, so that repeated requests for continuances can be vigorously resisted. Also, there are strategies your lawyer can use when the opposing counsel is chronically unprepared. These strategies include providing information proactively so that complaints about not having information can be combatted. There are also discovery resources (interrogatories) that help confine issues the other side can raise. By limiting the issues, you can minimize last-minute continuances. Discuss these strategies with your lawyer.

15.7 If I have to go to court, will I be put on the stand? Will there be a jury?

As mentioned earlier, in Illinois, divorce matters are heard before a judge only; juries do not hear divorces. Whether you will be put on the stand will depend upon the nature of the issues in dispute, the judge assigned to your case, and your attorney's strategy for your case. You need to confirm in advance of the court date whether you will likely have to testify so that you can prepare.

15.8 My lawyer told me I will have to testify and I am terrified. What can I expect?

The thought of testifying is frightening to many people. If you are called to testify, both your lawyer and your spouse's lawyer have the right to ask you questions. When your lawyer asks you questions, the procedure is called *direct examination* and when your spouse's lawyer asks you questions, it is called *cross-examination*. During your examination, whether direct or cross, you will likely hear both attorneys make objections. *Objections* are the procedure for controlling the evidence the other side attempts to present. If you hear an objection from either attorney, stop talking immediately and wait for the judge to rule on the objection. The judge will either "overrule" the objection and direct you to answer the question or, alternatively, the judge will "sustain" (agree with) the objection and direct the lawyer to ask another question.

If you are testifying, you may not look at your notes without permission of the judge. If you have notes that you may need to rely on, place them in a folder and take them to the witness stand but don't look at them unless the judge permits you to do so. Often, your notes can be looked at to *refresh your recollection,* which is a legal procedure to help a witness who can't remember. If you do forget something, your lawyer will ask you if your memory is exhausted. If the answer is yes, the attorney will ask you whether something might refresh your recollection. If you have notes that will help you, you may then look at the notes. Be aware, however, that the other side will then have a right to see your notes so make sure nothing confidential is included in them.

Again, although you will be nervous, try to stay calm so that you can accurately present the necessary evidence for your case. It always helps to do a rehearsal; ask your lawyer if he or she will do a practice run with you prior to the hearing. Also ask your lawyer the likely topics that the other side will cross-examine you on, and develop a strategy how to respond to those questions. Preparation always helps lower your stress and will make for a better result.

15.9 My lawyer told me to be in court for our *temporary hearing* next week. What's going to happen?

A *temporary hearing* determines such matters as who remains in the house while your divorce is pending, temporary parenting time, and temporary support. The procedure for a temporary hearing depends upon the county where your case was filed, the assigned judge, and whether temporary parenting issues are disputed. Many temporary hearings are held on the basis of written affidavits summarizing your income and expenses, and the arguments of the lawyers. Although you should plan to attend your temporary hearing, it is possible that the hearing will be held in the judge's chambers with only the judge and attorneys present.

Even if your temporary hearing is held in the judge's chambers, your presence at the hearing is still important. Your attorney may need additional information from you during the hearing, and last-minute negotiations to resolve temporary issues are not uncommon.

In some counties, your hearing will be one of numerous other hearings on the judge's calendar. You may find yourself in a courtroom with many other lawyers and their clients, all having matters scheduled before the court that day.

If you and your spouse disagree on temporary parental responsibility, you and other witnesses might be required to testify. If this is the case, meeting with your attorney in advance to fully prepare is very important. Talk to your lawyer about the procedure you should expect for the temporary hearing in your case.

15.10 A *pretrial conference* has been scheduled for my case. What happens at that hearing?

A *pretrial conference,* also known as a *settlement conference,* is an informal hearing, usually conducted in the judge's chambers. The parties are not present during this hearing, and the lawyers give the judge a memorandum summarizing the facts of the case and the contested issues. The divorcing parties are not present during this hearing because judges frequently want attorneys to candidly discuss the weaknesses of their cases, which is difficult for some lawyers with their client present. (As an aside, if your lawyer can't be candid with you about the weaknesses of your case, you should get another lawyer—promises of sunshine on a rainy day will cause more problems for you in the long run). At the conclusion of the hearing, the judge will make an informal recommendation designed to help the parties settle the case.

Make sure you have an opportunity to discuss the recommendation with your lawyer after the pretrial conference. The judge who made the recommendation is often the judge who will try the case. If the judge has assessed the case, it may be futile to proceed to trial. Ask your attorney whether the judge might look at the case differently if you try the case, and the cost and risks of proceeding despite an unfavorable recommendation.

15.11 Do I have to go to court if all of the issues in my case are settled?

Under Illinois law, a final court hearing is required even if you and your spouse have settled your case. At this hearing, the prove-up, the judge will review the agreement and make sure it is appropriate and conforms to the law. In most instances, only the spouse who filed the divorce complaint must attend. Sometimes, however, either the judge or the attorneys will insist that the other spouse appear as well, in order to clarify that he or she fully understands the terms of the agreement.

At the prove-up hearing the lawyers will give the judge a copy of your agreement and you (and your spouse if he or she attends) will be asked questions about the agreement. First, the lawyer will ask you some background questions about such things as the date of your marriage, and your children. Next, the lawyer will ask you whether irreconcilable differences caused the irretrievable breakdown of the marriage.

Finally, the highlights of the agreement will be covered, and your lawyer will make sure you understand the important provisions. For example, if you waive maintenance, the lawyer will make sure you understand the finality of the waiver and that you have an ability to support yourself. At the conclusion of the hearing, the lawyers will give the judge a number of documents to review, including your settlement agreement, the judgment for dissolution of marriage, support withholding orders, and QDROs.

15.12 Are there any rules about *courtroom etiquette* that I need to know?

Knowing a few tips about courtroom etiquette will make your experience easier:

- Dress comfortably yet respectfully. Avoid overly casual dress, lots of jewelry, revealing clothing, and extreme hairstyles.
- Be sure to turn off your cell phone.
- Be polite to the judge and opposing counsel.
- Maintain a proper reverential demeanor—the courtroom is a place of respect, not levity.
- Don't take beverages into the courtroom. Most courts have rules barring food and drink in courtrooms. If you need water, ask your lawyer.
- Don't chew gum.
- Don't talk aloud in the courtroom unless you're on the witness stand or being questioned by the judge.
- Stand up whenever the judge is entering or leaving the courtroom.

Although you may feel anxious initially, you'll likely feel more relaxed about the courtroom setting once your hearing gets underway.

15.13 What is the role of the *court clerk*?

The *court clerk* who sits in the courtroom is the administrative assistant to the judge. The clerk helps the judge keep track of the cases scheduled and manages all of the orders that are presented to the judge throughout the course of the court proceedings. If there is a trial, the clerk keeps track of all of the exhibits that are presented during the trial.

15.14 Will there be a *court reporter* present, and what will he or she do?

A *court reporter* is a professional trained to make an accurate record of the words spoken and documents offered into evidence during court proceedings. Some counties have the court reporter located outside of the courtroom and transmit the testimony via microphone. Some counties provide court reporters while other counties require the parties to hire private reporters to attend hearings.

A written transcript of a court proceeding may be purchased from the court reporter. If your case is appealed, the appellate court will use the transcript to review the facts of your case.

Some hearings or portions of hearings are held "off the record." This expression means that the court reporter is not making a record of what is being said. If there is a court reporter and the judge indicates a conversation is off the record, this means that the conversation has no evidentiary or procedural value and probably applies to a scheduling matter. If a hearing goes forward without a court reporter, there will be no formal record of that hearing and it will be difficult to appeal because of the lack of a transcript. If there is any chance a case might need to be appealed, ensure the presence of a court reporter.

15.15 Will I be able to talk to my attorney while we are in court?

During court proceedings your attorney must give his or her full attention to everything being said by the judge, witnesses, or your spouse's lawyer. For this reason, try to avoid talking with your lawyer when anyone else in the courtroom is speaking. Take pen and paper with you when you go to court. If your court proceeding is underway and your lawyer is listening to what is being said by others in the courtroom, write him or her a note with your questions or comments.

It is critical that your attorney hear each question asked by the other lawyer and all answers given by each witness. If your lawyer is chatting with you, he or she may miss making an important objection to inappropriate evidence. You can support your attorney by avoiding talking to him or her while a court hearing is in progress.

If your court hearing is lengthy, breaks will be taken. You can use this time to discuss with your attorney any questions or observations you have about the proceeding.

15.16 Besides meeting with my lawyer, is there anything else I should do to prepare for my upcoming trial?

Review your deposition and any information you provided in your discovery, such as answers to interrogatories. At trial, you may be asked some of the same questions. If you think you might give different answers at trial, discuss this with your lawyer. It is important that your attorney know in advance of trial whether any information you provided during the discovery process has changed.

15.17 I'm meeting with my lawyer to prepare for trial. How do I make the most of these meetings?

Meeting with your lawyer to prepare for your trial is important. It's been said that trial preparation is 90 percent perspiration and 10 percent inspiration. Preparation is hard work, but it can pay dividends. Come to the meeting prepared to discuss the following:

- The issues in your case
- Your desired outcome on each of the issues
- The questions you might be asked at trial by both lawyers
- The exhibits that will be offered into evidence during the trial
- The witnesses for your trial
- The status of negotiations

At some point prior to trial, you should meet with your lawyer to rehearse your direct examination as well.

15.18 My lawyer says that the law firm is busy with "trial preparation." What exactly is my lawyer doing to prepare for my trial?

Countless tasks are necessary to prepare your case for trial. These are just some of them:

- Developing arguments to be made on each of the contested issues
- Researching and reviewing the relevant law in your case

- Reviewing the facts of your case to determine which witnesses are best suited to testifying about them
- Reading and summarizing all witness depositions
- Reviewing, selecting, and preparing exhibits
- Researching evidence to support admission (or exclusion) of exhibits or testimony
- Preparing summary exhibits or charts
- Preparing questions for all witnesses
- Preparing an opening statement
- Determining the order of witnesses and all exhibits
- Interviewing and preparing all witnesses
- Preparing your file for the day in court, including preparing a trial notebook with essential information

Trials are often won or lost based upon the level of preparation. Trials are expensive largely due to the time necessary for thorough preparation. This cost must be kept in mind when evaluating settlement options.

15.19 My divorce is scheduled for trial. Does this mean there is no hope for a settlement?

Many cases are settled after a trial date is set. The setting of a trial date may cause you and your spouse to think about the risks and costs of going to trial. This can help you and your spouse focus on what is most important to you and lead you toward a negotiated settlement. Because the costs of preparing for and proceeding to trial are substantial, it is best to engage in settlement negotiations well in advance of your trial date.

15.20 Can I prevent my spouse from being in the courtroom?

No. Your spouse has a legal interest in the outcome of your divorce; he or she has a right to be present. Illinois courtrooms are open to the public. Consequently, it is not uncommon for persons not involved in your divorce to pass through the courtroom at various times simply because they have other business with the court.

15.21 Can I take a friend or family member with me to court?

Yes. Let your attorney know in advance if you intend to take someone to court with you. Some people important to you may be very emotional about your divorce or your spouse. Be sure to invite someone who is better able to focus attention on supporting you rather than on his or her own feelings. If your friend is also a witness in the case, that person cannot sit in the courtroom until after he or she testifies.

15.22 I want to do a great job testifying as a witness in my divorce trial. What are some tips?

Keep the following in mind to be a good witness on your own behalf:

- Tell the truth. This may not be always be comfortable, but it is critical if you want your testimony to be believed by the judge.

- Wait to consider your answer until the full question is asked. Take a breath and then answer.

- Take your time. You may be asked some questions that call for a thoughtful response. If you need a moment to reflect on an answer before you give it, allow yourself that time.

- If you don't understand a question or don't know the answer, be sure to say so.

- Slow down. It's easy to speed up our speech when we are anxious. Taking your time with your answers ensures that the judge hears you and that the court reporter can accurately record your testimony.

- If the question calls for a "yes" or "no" answer, simply say so. Then wait for the attorney to ask you the next question. If there is more you want to explain, remember that you have already told your attorney all the important facts and he or she will make sure you are allowed to give any testimony significant in your case. Witnesses who regularly volunteer information beyond the question asked draw objections and usually irritate the judge.

- Don't argue with the judge or the lawyers.
- Stop speaking if an objection is made by one of the lawyers. Wait until the judge has decided whether to allow you to answer.

15.23 Should I be worried about being cross-examined by my spouse's lawyer at trial?

If your case goes to trial, prepare to be asked some questions by your spouse's lawyer. Many of these questions will call for a simple "yes" or "no." If you are worried about particular questions, discuss your concerns with your attorney. Your lawyer can help you contemplate how you will respond to a particular line of questions. Try not to take the questions personally; the lawyer is doing his or her job. Remember that you are just doing your best to tell the truth about the facts.

Also remember that your attorney will have the ability to clarify your answers. After cross-examination, your lawyer will ask you questions called a *re-direct examination*. If you are boxed in on cross-examination, and disallowed the ability to explain your answer, your lawyer will allow you to explain during your re-direct examination.

15.24 What happens on the day of trial?

In any trial, the party who files the case is known as the *plaintiff* or the *petitioner*. The opposing party is known as the *defendant* or the *respondent*. Although no two trials are alike, the following steps will occur in most divorce trials:

- Attorneys may start by meeting with the judge in chambers to discuss procedural issues, such as how many witnesses will be called, how long the case will take to present, and when breaks might be taken. (Sometimes this meeting occurs the week before the trial at a final pretrial conference.)
- Attorneys give opening statements.
- Plaintiff's attorney calls plaintiff's witnesses to testify. Defendant's attorney may cross-examine each of them.

- Plaintiff's attorney may again examine the witnesses to clarify anything said on cross-examination (re-direct examination).

- Defendant's attorney calls defendant's witness to testify. Plaintiff's attorney may cross-examine each of them. Defendant's attorney may conduct a re-direct examination of the witness.

- Plaintiff's lawyer calls any *rebuttal witnesses,* that is, witnesses whose testimony contradicts the testimony of the defendant's witnesses. Defendant does not call any rebuttal witnesses.

- Closing arguments are made first by the plaintiff's attorney and then by the defendant's attorney. In some cases judges request written closing arguments that are usually filed with the judge after the testimony concludes.

15.25 Will the judge decide my case the day I go to court?

Possibly. Often, however, there is so much information from the trial for the judge to consider that it is not possible for the judge to give an immediate ruling.

The judge may want to review documents, review the law, perform calculations, review his or her notes, and give thoughtful consideration to the issues to be decided. For this reason, it may be days, weeks, or, in some cases, even longer before a ruling is made.

When a judge does not make a ruling immediately upon the conclusion of a trial, it is said that the case has been "taken under advisement." The judge will rule several weeks (and in some cases months) after the conclusion of the trial.

15.26 I received my ruling and the judge made a simple mistake. Is there anything I can do to correct the mistake short of a full appeal?

Within thirty days after the entry of the court's judgment, either party can file a *posttrial motion* requesting that the judge change all or a part of the ruling based upon a mistake or other reasons. Often, this motion is called a *motion to reconsider*. It is rare that a judge will change his or her mind, but if a clear mistake is pointed out, the judge may correct it at that time.

16

The Appeals Process

At the conclusion of the case, either party may appeal the trial court's decision. An appeal is filed and heard by the appellate court in the district where your case is heard. There are five appellate court districts, located throughout the state. The Illinois Supreme Court in Springfield is also an *appellate court,* the highest court in the state.

The appellate process involves the preparation and filing of *appellate briefs,* which are lengthy documents summarizing the facts and the legal arguments for the appellate court to review. The person appealing (called the *appellant*) argues that the trial court made a mistake, either by misunderstanding the facts of the case or misapplying the law. The person responding to the appeal (called the *appellee*) files a brief arguing why the trial court decision was appropriate.

A panel of three appellate court justices will review the briefs. If the arguments are clear and the justices have no questions, they will issue a written decision, known as an *opinion.* Sometimes the justices have questions. In that event, they will schedule *oral arguments.* The oral argument is conducted at the appellate court and the attorneys appear personally before the appellate justices, give a presentation, and answer the justice's questions. The appellate opinion usually follows shortly after the oral argument. After the opinion is issued, either party may ask the Supreme Court to review the decision. The Supreme Court is not required to review all cases decided and can pick and choose those cases it will agree to consider.

Appellate court procedure is very different from the procedure in the trial court. Also, the legal skills necessary to handle an appeal are different from those skills used by lawyers in the trial court. An appellate lawyer must have extraordinary research and writing skills. The lawyer must also have the ability to present your case clearly and concisely in an oral argument. If you do consider an appeal, make sure you seek out a lawyer who regularly handles appeals.

16.1 How much time after my divorce do I have to file an appeal?

You must file an appeal within thirty days of the final order you wish to appeal. Because your attorney may also recommend filing posttrial motions following your trial, discuss the timing of your appeal with your lawyer as soon as you have received the judge's ruling.

16.2 Can I appeal a temporary order?

No. Typically, only final orders may be appealed. That means the appellate court cannot consider trial court rulings on temporary matters such as temporary support. There are some limited exceptions to this rule but by and large an appeal can only be filed at the end of the case.

16.3 What parts of the final judgment can be appealed?

You don't need to appeal all aspects of the court's ruling, only those aspects that may be considered improper. For example, you may be satisfied with the ruling on parenting time and decision making but not with the amount of child support. You would just appeal the issue of child support. Your former spouse, however, may appeal other issues (such as parental responsibilities in this instance). Also, procedural issues can be appealed. Perhaps your attorney asked for a continuance because of a missing witness and the judge denied the motion. That denial of the continuance could be raised in the appeal. If the trial judge acted in a way to deprive you of a fair trial, you can raise that issue in the appellate court as well.

16.4   How will I know what issues to appeal?

Your attorney may counsel you to file an appeal on certain issues of your case; you may also ask your lawyer whether there is a legitimate basis for an appeal of any decision you believe is wrong. Talk to your attorney regarding the decisions most dissatisfying to you. Your lawyer can advise which issues have the greatest likelihood of success on appeal, in light of the facts of your case and Illinois law.

16.5   When should an appeal be filed?

An appeal should be filed only after careful consultation with your lawyer when you believe that the judge has made a serious error under the law or the facts of your case. Among the factors you and your attorney should discuss are:

- Whether the judge had the authority under the law to make the decisions set forth in your decree
- The likelihood of the success of your appeal
- The risk that an appeal by you will encourage an appeal by your former spouse
- The cost of the appeal
- The length of time an appeal can be expected to take
- The impact of a delay in the case during the appeal

The deadline for filing an appeal is thirty days from the date that a final order is entered in your case. It is important that you are clear about the deadline that applies in your case, so talk to your attorney at once if you are thinking about an appeal. Once the deadline has passed, you can't change your mind and file an appeal at that point.

16.6   Are there any disadvantages to filing an appeal?

There can be disadvantages to filing an appeal, including:

- Uncertainty as to the outcome
- Increased attorney fees and costs
- The risks of a worse outcome on appeal than you received at trial

- Prolonged conflict between you and your former spouse
- Risk of a second trial occurring after the appeal
- Delay in obtaining closure and moving forward with your life

16.7   Is an attorney necessary to appeal?

The appeals process is very detailed and specific, with set deadlines and specific court rules. Also, the appellate court is more interested in legal arguments. Most laypeople are not trained in the skills necessary to research and write these arguments. Given the complex nature of the appellate process, you should have an attorney if you intend to file an appeal. The appellate court is much less forgiving than the trial court, which has accommodated people who have chosen to represent themselves.

16.8   How long does the appeals process usually take?

An appeal can take anywhere from several months to well over a year. Illinois rules require that appeals regarding parental responsibility issues be accelerated and those are resolved in a few months. Appeals involving solely financial issues may last up to a year. An appeal may also result in the appellate court requiring further proceedings by the trial court. In other words, the appellate court might send the case back to the trial court with instructions to re-decide certain issues. This will result in further delay.

16.9   What are the steps in the appeals process?

There are many steps your lawyer will take on your behalf in the appeals process, including:

- Identifying the issues to be appealed
- Filing a notice with the court of your intent to appeal
- Obtaining the necessary court documents and trial exhibits to send to the appellate court

- Obtaining a transcript of the trial, a written copy of testimony by witnesses and statements by the judge and the lawyers made in the presence of the court reporter

- Performing legal research to support your arguments on appeal

- Preparing and filing a document known as a *brief,* which sets forth the facts of the case and relevant law, complete with citations to court transcript, court documents, and prior cases

- Making an oral argument before the judges of the appellate court

16.10 Is filing and pursuing an appeal expensive?

Yes. In addition to filing fees and lawyer fees, there is likely to be a substantial cost for the preparation of the transcript of the trial testimony.

16.11 If I do not file an appeal, can I ever go back to court to change my decree?

Certain aspects of a decree are not modifiable, such as the division of property and debts or the award of attorney fees. Other parts of your decree, such as support or matters regarding the children, may be modified if there has been a "substantial change in circumstances." Any issue related to children is always modifiable.

A modification of parental responsibility for minor children will also require you to show that the change would be in their best interest. Parenting time, parental decision making, relocations, child support, and all other issues related to children are all subject to modification when appropriate.

If your decree did not provide for maintenance, or if it ordered that the maintenance be non-modifiable, it is unlikely that you will be able to change it. On the other hand, if your agreement does not specifically limit your ability to modify it, you may be able to petition the court for a change in the amount you are receiving or paying. Again, you must prove that there has been a change in circumstances. If you believe that you have a basis for a modification of your divorce decree, consult with your attorney.

In Closing

I hope that you have found this book helpful. Remember, nothing replaces the advice of an experienced divorce lawyer. The information contained in this book can't be used as a substitute for that advice. Each case is different and although I have given you an overview of the law generally, things are much more complex in real-world application.

You can survive divorce! People not only survive, but many flourish by escaping negative or toxic relationships. Focus on a positive future. Think about possibilities and opportunities rather than dashed dreams or unfulfilled promises. Don't focus on the security of your existing relationship if it is unhealthy. Security is an illusion, and the only real security is your ability to think clearly and live in a healthy and positive emotional environment.

Undoubtedly, divorce sucks. A client once asked why it was so awful. I thought about it and responded that I suppose, as a society, we don't want to make the process too pleasant for fear that more people will divorce. In any event, the pain of divorce is a fact of life, and it is better dealt with head on, rather than trying to deny it or run from it. The best way out of a problem is straight through it.

A judge once compared divorce to a death. Once an organism dies, it will start to decompose. The same applies to a relationship. Once you have concluded that the marriage is dead, you must leave it behind. Grieve its loss so that you can move on.

I have spent my entire career helping people through divorce. I strive to make each one a successful divorce. This is possible. Be smart, be reasonable, and keep your emotions in check. Self-pity will get you nowhere. Consider your divorce as an opportunity to rebuild your life in a more positive and healthy manner. And don't forget...being happy is the best revenge!

Resources

American Academy of Matrimonial Lawyers (AAML)
www.aaml.org

AAML is an organization of elite family law lawyers who must go through a grueling examination process before they are accepted as fellows. Its website offers a broad range of information on all family law–related matters. It has a library where you can access current and past issues of its journal and newsletter, and it also offers videos on how to navigate the divorce process. There is also a feature that allows you to search for lawyers who are fellows of AAML.

Best Lawyers
www.bestlawyers.com

Inclusion in this group is entirely based on peer review. The website offers a comprehensive search function to find a lawyer in your area to fit your specific needs.

Child Support Services
Phone: (800) 447-4278

https://online.hfs.illinois.gov/online/entry-flow.htm?execution =e1s1

As part of Healthcare and Family Services, this site provides multiple resources to help parents understand child support, including forms and brochures on multiple topics and information. The website offers directions on how to apply for services, calculate child support, and enforce existing child support obligations. It is a good starting point for parents, attorneys, and others who have questions about the process, and it can direct you to more-specific resources if necessary.

Cook County Clerk of the Circuit Court
www.cookcountyclerkofcourt.org
This website is designed to guide self-represented (*pro se*) parties through family law matters in Cook County. Although it is county-specific, it does provide general information including links to outside resources.

Credit reports
www.annualcreditreport.com
Every twelve months, you are entitled to receive a free copy of your credit report. This is the official site, as directed by the Federal Trade Commission, to assist consumers in obtaining their report.

Illinois Coalition Against Domestic Violence
Phone: (877) 863-6338
www.ilcadv.org
The purpose of the Illinois Coalition Against Domestic Violence is to eliminate violence against women and their children; to promote the eradication of domestic violence across the state of Illinois; to ensure the safety of survivors, their access to services, and their freedom of choice; to hold abusers accountable for the violence they perpetrate; and to encourage the development of victim-sensitive laws, policies, and procedures across all systems that impact survivors of domestic violence. Their website offers numerous resources.

Illinois Legal Aid Online
www.IllinoisLegalAid.org
This nonprofit group provides information to help the public and *pro se* litigants navigate the legal system. Founded in 2001, Illinois Legal Aid Online uses technology and local self-help centers to make information as accessible as possible. The group even has downloadable applications for mobile devices. It operates a Spanish-language companion site and is developing an app for that as well.

Illinois Marriage and Dissolution of Marriage Act
www.ilga.gov/legislation/ilcs/ilcs3.asp?ActID=2086&ChapterID=59
The text of the *Illinois Marriage and Dissolution of Marriage Act* is available at this web address.

Illinois State Bar Association

www.illinoislawyerfinder.com/articles/you-and-the-law/family/marriage-and-divorce

The Illinois State Bar Association (ISBA) operates this site to assist people in finding a family law lawyer. It provides background information about hiring a lawyer, seeking custody, parenting time and decision-making rights, grounds for annulment, and a host of other issues. The ISBA has been a force in the legal community since 1877 and currently has more than 30,000 members.

Illinois State Disbursement Unit

Phone: (877) 225-7077
www.ilsdu.com
P.O. Box 5921
Carol Stream, IL 60197-5921

The Illinois State Disbursement Unit (SDU) is a division of Child Support Services. The SDU is the central unit where all support payments are sent, processed, and distributed. At this website, you can view recently made payments, obtain forms to authorize payments to be directly deposited into your bank account, and change your address, among other services. This website can help answer any support-related questions or concerns you may have.

Internal Revenue Service

www.irs.gov/publications/p504

The tax implications of divorce can be complicated, and the IRS provides a guidebook on how to handle those particular issues: "Publication 504 – Divorced or Separated Individuals." It addresses exemptions, maintenance, property settlements, and the costs of getting divorced, among other related topics.

Parenting Communication Assistance

www.ourfamilywizard.com

For a fee, this site provides tools for parents to better communicate with each other regarding parenting issues. It has calendars, message boards, expense logs, and other devices that both parents can access.

Social Security Administration
www.ssa.gov
Divorce can have an impact on how Social Security benefits are received and distributed. This site provides information on what benefits are available to former spouses, eligibility requirements, and application forms.

Southern Illinois University School of Law
The Self-Help Legal Center
https://law.siu.edu/lawlib/general/selfhelp.htm
This site offers downloadable forms and information regarding various divorce processes throughout the state.

U.S. Department of Health and Human Services
www.acf.hhs.gov/programs/css
This is the site of Federal Office of Child Support Enforcement–under the Office of the Administration for Children and Families, which is under the U.S. Department of Health and Human Services. Its mission is primarily to assist local agencies in their child support enforcement programs, and information is available for parents looking to better understand the process. A handbook can be found on the website at (www.acf. hhs.gov/programs/css/resource/handbook-on-child-support-enforcement).

U.S. Department of State
https://travel.state.gov/content/travel/en/International-Parental-Child-Abduction.html
This website, operated by the United States Department of State, provides resources and information about international parental kidnappings. The website offers directions on how to open a parental kidnapping case and country-specific information for those who know where their child has been taken. The Office of Children's Issues has a toll-free number available twenty-four hours a day for emergency situations in which the child is in the process of being abducted but is not yet out of the country.

For updates on resources in this list visit
(www.peskindlaw.com/legal-updates).

Glossary

affidavit: A written statement of facts made under oath and signed before a notary public. Affidavits are used primarily when there will not be a hearing in open court with live testimony. The attorney will prepare an affidavit to present relevant facts. Affidavits may be signed by the parties or in some cases by witnesses. The person signing the affidavit may be referred to as the *affiant.*

alimony: Court-ordered spousal support payments from one party to another, often to enable the recipient spouse to become economically independent. In Illinois this type of spousal support is known as *maintenance.*

allegation: A statement that one party claims is true.

answer: A written response to the petition for divorce. It serves to admit or deny the allegations in the complaint and may also make claims against the opposing party. This is sometimes called a *responsive pleading.* An answer should be filed within thirty days of either (a) the complaint being served by the sheriff or (b) the defendant's voluntary appearance being filed with the court.

appeal: The process by which a higher court reviews the decision of a lower court.

appearance: An appearance is a document that is filed with the court, and submits you to the power of the court. Once filed, the court can take action against you without the need to have the sheriff or process server serve you with the papers.

appellant: The person requesting the appeal.

appellate brief: The lengthy documents summarizing the facts and the legal arguments for the appellate court to review.

221

appellee: The person defending the appeal.

arbitration: The act of submitting a contested case to a "private judge" to resolve the issues.

arrearage: The amount of unpaid back child support due to a parent or unpaid maintenance due to a former spouse.

associate attorney: A lawyer with less experience than senior lawyers but a skilled lawyer nevertheless. Usually, the more experienced lawyer trains and mentors these junior lawyers, who are fully capable of handling your case.

chambers: The judge's office.

child relocation: A proceeding seeking permission of the court for a parent to move with the children.

child representative: An attorney who investigates and advocates for the best interest of the child in court, but does not testify as a witness or give an opinion.

child support: Financial support for a child paid by the noncustodial parent to the custodial parent.

collaborative divorce: An agreement by the parties to avoid resolving their dispute in court using trained lawyers and neutral facilitators.

complaint: The first document filed with the clerk of the court in an action for divorce, separation, or paternity. The complaint sets forth the facts on which the requested relief is based.

consideration: A bargained-for exchange.

contempt of court: The willful and intentional failure of a party to comply with a court order, judgment, or decree. Contempt may be punishable by a fine or jail.

contested case: Any case in which the parties cannot reach an agreement. A contested case will result in a trial to have the judge decide disputed issues.

court clerk: The administrative assistant to the judge.

court order: A court-issued document setting forth the judge's orders. An order can be issued based upon the parties' agreement or the judge's decision. An order may require the parties to perform certain acts or set forth their rights and responsibilities. An order is put in writing, signed by the judge, and filed with the court.

Glossary

court order acceptable for processing: This order acts like a QDRO, transferring to the former spouse his or her benefits directly.

court reporter: A professional trained to make an accurate record of the words spoken and documents offered into evidence during court proceedings.

cross-examination: The questioning of a witness by the opposing counsel during trial or at a deposition, in response to questions asked by the other lawyer.

decision-making rights: A court decree that grants one or both parents rights to decide issues related to the children's religious training, health, education, and extracurricular participation.

declaration of invalidity of marriage: Also known as an *annulment*. A proceeding to avoid the effect of a marriage based upon certain limited factors.

decree of dissolution: A final court order dissolving the marriage, dividing property and debts, ordering support, and entering other orders regarding finances and the minor children.

defendant: The responding party to a divorce; the party who did not file the complaint initiating the divorce.

defined benefit plan: Usually a pension, this plan pays the employee a monthly payment at some predetermined future date, usually after he or she retires.

deposition: A witness's testimony taken out of court, under oath, and in the presence of lawyers and a court reporter. If a person gives a different testimony at the time of trial, he or she can be impeached with the deposition testimony; that is, statements made at a deposition can be used to show untruthfulness if a different answer is given at trial.

direct examination: The initial questioning of a witness in court by the lawyer who called him or her to the stand.

discovery: A process used by attorneys to discover information from the opposing party for the purpose of fully assessing a case for settlement or trial. Types of discovery include interrogatories, requests for production of documents, and requests for admissions.

dissipation of marital assets: If one of the parties uses marital assets or income for an improper purpose during a period of time that the marriage is breaking down.

dissolution: The act of terminating or dissolving a marriage.

domestic support obligation: An order from a family court regarding child support, maintenance, or property. It is not dischargeable in bankruptcy and a person ordered to pay cannot avoid the obligation through bankruptcy.

domestic violence order of protection: A court order that protects a victim of domestic violence and allows the protected party to contact police if violated. Violation of the order results in criminal prosecution.

equitable distribution of property: The method by which real and personal property and debts are divided in a divorce. Equitable doesn't always mean equal.

exhibits: Physical evidence (documents, photographs, for example) that a court can consider in deciding any issues at a trial or a hearing.

ex parte: Usually in reference to a motion, the term used to describe an appearance of only one party before the judge, without the other party being present. For example, an *ex parte* restraining order may be granted immediately after the filing of a complaint for divorce.

financial affidavit: A statewide form created by the Illinois Supreme Court that lists a party's income, expenses, debts, and property.

flat fee: A fixed amount for the legal services provided.

guardian *ad litem* (GAL): A lawyer appointed by court to conduct an investigation and report to the judge regarding the children's best interest.

hearing: Any proceeding before the court for the purpose of resolving disputed issues between the parties through presentation of testimony, affidavits, exhibits, or argument.

hold-harmless clause: A term in a court order that requires one party to assume responsibility for a debt and to protect the other spouse from any loss or expense in connection with it, as in to "hold harmless from liability."

in camera interview: An interview by a judge of a child in a contested parental responsibility action.

initial consultation: The first meeting between a client and a potential lawyer.

injunction: A court order requiring a party to refrain from certain conduct.

Glossary

innocent spouse relief: This refers to a method of obtaining relief from the Internal Revenue Service for taxes owed as a result of a joint income tax return filed during your marriage.

interrogatories: Written questions sent from one party to the other that are used to obtain facts or opinions related to the divorce.

irreconcilable differences: The only basis for an Illinois divorce. Illinois recognizes no other grounds for a divorce.

judgment for dissolution of marriage: The final divorce decree signed by the judge.

legal separation: A proceeding to legally separate involves court orders allocating parental responsibility and financial orders for a period that the parties are legally separated. Similar to a divorce.

litigation budget: A tool developed by your lawyer to help you understand the nature of the services, time spent, and possible overall costs anticipated in your divorce. This is particularly useful if your case is complex and you are anticipating substantial legal fees.

maintenance: Spousal support, which is usually determined by formula and paid for a duration based upon the length of the marriage. Also known as *alimony*.

marital balance sheet: An inventory of marital assets and debts, often used to assist in settlement negotiations.

marital property: If property belongs to the marital estate, it is considered marital property and is subject to division. The law presumes that all property acquired by either party during the marriage is marital property.

marital settlement agreement: A contract setting forth the terms of your divorce agreement. It covers topics such as property division, maintenance, child support, attorney fees, and all related matters.

mediation: A process by which a neutral third party facilitates negotiations between the divorcing parties on a wide range of issues. In Illinois, a divorce that involves children requires mediation if parents cannot agree on parenting time and decision-making rights.

motion: A written application to the court for relief, such as temporary child support, parenting time, decision-making rights, or restraining orders.

motion to compel: A request made to force compliance from a spouse.

motion to reconsider: Another name for a posttrial motion in which you ask the judge to modify his or her ruling on a matter.

negotiation: A process that allows you and your spouse to resolve your disputed issues and reach an agreement without submitting the case to the judge.

nesting arrangement: Where instead of the children circulating between the parents' homes, the parents take turns being with the children at the marital home.

nonmarital property: Property owned prior to the marriage and that remains the exclusive property of the party who owns it.

notice of hearing: A written statement sent to the opposing lawyer or spouse listing the date and place of a hearing and the nature of the matters that will be heard by the court.

oral argument: Conducted at the appellate court, the attorneys appear personally before the appellate justices to give a presentation on their case and answer the justice's questions.

order of protection: A court order that offers protections to a spouse and children in a domestic violence situation.

paralegal: A trained legal professional who provides support for you and your lawyer, sometimes called a *legal assistant.*

parental responsibility: Formerly referred to as *child custody.* This term encapsulates the allocation of parental decision making and parenting time with the children.

parenting plan: This document sets forth the terms concerning parenting decision making, parenting time, and the parents' respective rights and responsibilities with regard to the children.

parenting time: The time a child spends with either parent, formerly known as *visitation.*

party: The person in a legal action whose rights or interests will be affected by the divorce. For example, in a divorce the parties include the wife and husband.

personal jurisdiction: The court's power over a defendant.

petition: A written request asking the court for relief, similar to a motion.

Glossary

petitioner: The term used to refer to the plaintiff or person who files the complaint seeking a divorce.

petition for dissolution of marriage: The initiating document of an Illinois divorce proceeding.

petition for order to show cause: Written application to the court to hold another person in contempt of court for violating or failing to comply with a current court order.

pleadings: Documents filed with the court seeking a court order.

postnuptial agreement: A contract between married spouses to resolve future financial issues in the event of a later divorce.

posttrial motion: A written request that the judge change all or part of a ruling based upon a mistake or other reasons.

prenuptial agreement: A contract between parties contemplating a marriage to resolve any financial issues in advance of the marriage, in the event of a later divorce or death.

pretrial conference: An informal meeting that allows the lawyers to discuss with the judge the contested issues, soliciting how the judge might rule if the issues were presented at trial.

pro se: An individual who represents himself in court as opposed to having a lawyer to do so.

process server: A person authorized to server legal papers, typically on a defendant in a case.

property settlement: A property settlement is an agreement to allocate the parties marital property. It is usually contained in the parties' marital settlement agreement.

protective order: A court order restricting the dissemination of information disclosed in a divorce or other civil proceeding.

prove-up: A short hearing that allows the judge to review the terms of the agreement and ensure that the agreement is not unconscionable.

qualified domestic relations order (QDRO): A type of court order that provides for direct payment from a retirement account to a former spouse.

qualified Illinois domestic relations order (QILDRO): A court order that allows access to the pensions of Illinois government employees who are dividing their pensions as a result of a divorce. These orders operate very similar to a QDRO. Under a QILDRO, the plan administrator is ordered to transfer a portion of the employee's retirement benefit to a divorced spouse.

qualified medical child support order (QMCSO): An order that enables a parent to obtain medical information for a child covered by his or her spouse's group insurance plan.

refresh your recollection: A legal procedure to help a witness on the stand who can't remember something.

request for production of documents: A written request for documents sent from one party to the other during the discovery process.

respondent: The term used to refer to the *defendant* or person who responds to a complaint seeking a divorce.

retainer: A sum paid to your lawyer in advance for services to be performed and costs to be incurred in your divorce.

sequester: To order prospective witnesses out of the courtroom until they have concluded giving their testimony.

setoff: A debt or financial obligation of one spouse that is deducted from the debt or financial obligation of the other spouse.

settlement: The agreed resolution of disputed issues.

settlement conference: Also known as a *four-way conference,* this is a meeting held with you, your spouse, and both lawyers with the intention of negotiating the terms of your divorce.

spoliation of evidence: Where a party improperly destroys evidence.

stipulation: An agreement reached between parties or an agreement by their attorneys.

subpoena: A document delivered to a person or witness that requires him or her to appear in court, appear for a deposition, or produce documents. Failure to comply could result in punishment by the court. A subpoena requesting documents is called a *subpoena duces tecum.*

temporary hearing: This determines matters that must be addressed while your divorce is pending, such as who remains in the house, temporary parenting time, and temporary support. Orders entered in these hearings are not the final decisions.

temporary restraining order (TRO): An order of the court prohibiting a party from certain behavior. For example, a temporary restraining order may order a person not to transfer any funds during a pending divorce action.

Glossary

trial: A formal court hearing in which the judge will decide disputed issues raised by the parties' pleadings.

trial retainer: A sum of money paid on your account when it appears your case may not settle and will likely proceed to trial.

unconscionable: The term used to describe an agreement that is outrageous or oppressive.

under advisement: A term used to describe the status of a case, usually after a court hearing on a motion or a trial, when the judge has not yet made a decision.

Index

Numbers
401(k) plans, 16, 138, 163, 170, 172, 173, 175, 176, 178

A
abuse, 97, 98, 114, 117, 193
  background information, 88
  court records, 115
  criminal records, 115
  damaged property, 115
  emotional, 88
  evidence, 88, 89
  financial, 88
  history, 88
  medical records, 115
  medical treatments, 89
  nature of, 88
  photographs of damaged property, 115
  photographs of injuries, 115
  physical, 88, 98
  police reports, 89, 115
  sexual, 88, 114
  statements of admission, 89
  threatening letters, e-mails, voicemails, 114, 115
  traffic records, 115
  types, 88
  verbal, 88
  witnesses, 89
account statements, 58

accountants, 53, 54
  fees and costs, 192
accounts receivable, 163
addiction, 27
administrative costs, 53
administrative orders or forms, 19
advanced degrees, 164
affidavits, 129, 199
airplanes, 16
alcohol abuse, 89, 114, 115
alimony, 9, 139
  see also maintenance
allocation of parental responsibilities,
  see parental responsibility
alternative dispute resource, 83
American Academy of Matrimonial Law, 33
American Bar Association (ABA), 176
anger, 31
anger management classes, 114
annuities, 163
annulment, 5, 6
antenuptial agreement, 182
anxiety, 23, 29
appeals process, 209–216, 213
  arguments, 213
  court rules, 212

deadlines, 211, 212
disadvantages, 211
fees and costs, 211, 213
filing notice, 212
issues to appeal, 211
oral arguments, 213
steps, 212
when to file, 211
appearance, 11
appellant, 209
appellate briefs, 209
appellate court, 42, 202, 209,
    212
appellate court procedures,
    210
appellee, 209
appraisers, 53, 54
    fees and costs, 192
arbitration, 83
arbitrator, 83
arguments, 196, 197, 199, 203
    during an appeal, 209
    being present for, 197
arrearages of child support,
    137
art or antiques, 163
assets, 10, 16, 22, 54, 84, 147,
    163
    division, 5
    evaluation, 3, 54
    hiding, 55, 165
    trading, 152
associate attorney, 34, 50, 59
    benefits in working with,
        59
    fees and costs, 59
attorney fees and costs, 13,
    15, 17, 19, 38, 47–60, 137,
    213
    interim, 13
    tax deductions, 192
attorney general, 137
attorney-client privilege, 39
attorneys, 32–46
    changing, 34, 44
    for children, 41
    choosing, 32
    communication with, 44, 55,

57
conflict of interest, 35, 75
courtroom experience, 38
diligence, 52
disadvantages to changing,
    45, 46
experience, 50
free consultations, 33
hourly rates, 50, 52
initial consultation, 32, 34,
    35, 37, 38, 39
interviewing, 2, 33, 34
itemized statements, 48, 52,
    53, 59
limited-scope
    representation, 42
malpractice insurance, 35
not returning phone calls or
    e-mails, 44, 45
recommendations, 33
referrals, 2
reputation, 50
responsibilities, 39
scope of representation, 52
taking children to meetings
    with, 42
testimonials, 33
website, 58
working with, 32–46
automatic stay order, 90, 167,
    168

B

bailiff, 196
bank accounts, 16, 62, 91
bankruptcy, 54, 149, 160, 167,
    168, 169
base pay, 126
benefits, 170–181
Best Lawyers, 33
boats, 163
bonus income, 126, 128
briefs, 213
business evaluators, 54, 162
business income, 126
business interests, 16, 155
businesses, 38, 40, 41, 84,
    162
    evaluation, 54, 55

Index

valuations, 169

C

cabins, 16
campers, 16
capital gains tax, 159, 188, 189, 191
Carrad, David Clayton, 176
cash businesses, 128
certified public accountant (CPA), 188
chambers, 109, 196, 197, 199, 206
change in circumstances, 213
changing attorneys, 34
check registers, 146
Chicago Public Schools pensions, 178
child, children, 37, 40, 54
abduction, 92, 114
academic performance, 133
anxiety, 42, 104, 121, 122
see also child support
claiming as dependents, 191
college expenses, 15, 133
counseling, 24
court-ordered counseling, 105
day care providers, 107
depression, 24
developmental needs, 126
developmental stages, 110
disabled, 132
educational needs, 96, 118
effect of the divorce, 95
emergency situations, 112
emotional trauma, 28
exposure to details of divorce, 105
exposure to extramarital relationships, 106
extended family, 118
extracurricular activities, 96, 131
financial resources, 133
grants or scholarships, 133
health care, 96, 112, 131
health insurance, 15, 131, 170, 171
Illinois State Disbursement Unit, 134, 135
international travel, 120
kidnapping, 92, 114
marital home, 158
medical expenses, 126, 134
medical insurance, 134, 172
medical needs, 126
medical records, 112
parental roles chart, 99, 100
parent's financial responsibilities, 131
passports, 92, 93
personality, 110
physical needs, 126
preferences, 97, 111
psychologist, 23, 107, 113
religious training, 96
relocation, 15, 112, 118
removal from state, 90, 92
restricting access, 113
safety concerns, 113, 121, 122
school counselors, 24
school events, 120, 121
school fees, 131
school staff, 121
security, 95, 102, 104, 112
speaking to about divorce, 23
speaking to attorney, 110
speaking to judge, 109
special needs, 131
standard of living, 128, 132, 133
support groups, 24
taking to meetings with attorney, 42
tax exemptions, 15, 16
teachers, 107, 121
therapists, 23, 24
transportation issues, 112
travel inquiries, 112
at trial, 105
tuition, 133

vacations out of state, 92, 120
child abuse, 54
child custody,
see allocation of parental responsibilities, parenting time, parental responsibility
child dependency exemption, 191
child psychologist, 107
child representative, 41, 43, 109, 110
role, 111
child support, 9, 12, 15, 19, 36, 37, 81, 101, 124–138, 145, 168, 181, 192, 213
effect of having live-in partner, 136
arrearages, 137
calculating, 124
collections, 137
court-ordered, 127
deviations from guidelines, 125, 126
enforcement, 136, 137
guidelines, 125
HFS online calculator, 125
IRS Form 8332, 192
maintenance, 136
modifications, 125, 192
non-court-ordered, 127
permanent, 125
refusal to pay, 136, 178
remarriage, 136
special needs, 132
support-withholding orders, 135
taxes, 130, 189
temporary, 125, 129
trusts, 135
waiving, 129
withholding from wages, 134, 135
child support credit, 126
child support withholding orders, 19
child tax credit, 191

child-care expenses, 15
child-care tax credit, 192
Civil Service Retirement System, 177
civil unions, 6
claiming child/children as dependents, 191
clergy members, 26
clerk of the circuit court, 89
clerk of the court, 2, 4, 8, 10, 49
clerk of the tribal court, 9
clinical psychologist, 116
closing argument, 3, 207
COBRA (Consolidated Omnibus Budget Reconciliation Act of 1985), 170, 171
cohabitation with live-in partner, 9
collaborative law, 75
collections, 16, 163
evaluation, 54
college expenses, 15, 37, 132, 181
commercial property, 16
commingled assets, 153
commissions, 128
communication
with mediation, 78
with negotiations, 78
between spouses, 101, 116, 121
with your attorney, 14, 25, 27, 44, 59, 195
Complete QDRO Handbook, The, 176
conferences, 3, 40
with judge, 3
confidentiality, 23, 38, 52, 56, 58
conflict management, 38
conflict of interest, 18
consideration, 186
consultation fees, 37
consumer reporting companies, 166
contempt of court, 136

Index

contested custody, 107
contested divorce cases, 195
contested issues, 3, 55
continuances, 167, 197, 210
 denials, 210
continuing conjugal
 relationship, 148
contract law, 186
coping with stress, 22–31
copying fees, 52, 53
corporate distributions, 145
corporate tax returns, 146
counseling, 5, 24, 26, 27, 28,
 81
court,
 see trial, going to trial
court appearances, 40, 108,
 194, 195
 meeting with attorney prior
 to, 195
court assistants, 89
court clerk, 201
 role, 201
court dates, 2, 43, 195
 continuances, 197
court documents, 212
court hearings, 76, 194
 notice to appear, 196
court order acceptable for
 processing (COAP), 177
court orders, 12, 93, 103, 117,
 173, 189
court reporter, 62, 63, 68, 73,
 110, 201, 213
 fees and costs, 53, 65
court rules, 39
court security, 196
courtroom, 30, 105, 194, 196,
 201, 205
courtroom etiquette, 194, 201
credit card companies, 166,
 169
credit cards, 2, 57
credit reports, 138, 166
 free annual, 166, 167
criminal sanctions, 190
criminal prosecution, 138
cross-examination, 3, 111, 194,
 198, 206, 207

D

dating during divorce
 proceedings, 106
deadlines, 40, 195
death benefit, 183
debts, 63, 84, 142
decision-making rights, 12, 13,
 15, 37, 70, 88, 89, 97, 98, 99,
 102, 103, 105, 106, 107, 111,
 112, 114, 210
 emergency situations, 120
 medical records, 120
 school records, 120
declaration of invalidity of
 marriage, 5, 6
default orders, 12
defendant, 206
 witnesses, 207
defined benefit plan, 163, 172,
 173, 174, 175, 176, 178, 180
defined contribution accounts,
 138
delayed education, 141
denial, 31
Department of Agriculture,
 166
depositions, 29, 40, 54, 62, 63,
 65, 203
 copies, 73
 fees for copies, 73
 format, 69
 giving incorrect information,
 70
 judge's review, 69
 preparation for, 29, 68, 69,
 70
 protocols, 69
 purpose, 68
 questions asked, 70
 reviewing, 69
 reviewing documents, 71
 third parties, 146
 transcripts, 30, 63
 witnesses, 68, 72
depression, 24, 26, 31
developmental needs, 126
direct examination, 3, 198,

203
disability income, 141
disclosing intimate
    information, 23
discovery, 3, 17, 36, 40, 61–73,
    146, 165, 166, 197, 203
    extensions, 66
    medical records, 66
    overview, 61, 62
    responses, 43, 66
    types, 62, 64
    witnesses, 61
dissipation of marital assets,
    161
dividends, 145
divorce coaches, 26, 27, 66
divorce decree, 19
    see also judgment of
    dissolution of marriage
divorce expense reduction,
    58
divorce issues checklist,
    15–17
divorce law, 23, 42
divorce process, 1–21
    fees and costs, 49, 50
    steps, 1–4
    steps in filing, 10
divorce support groups, 26
documents, 58
    discovery, 61
    domestic violence, 115
    financial, 17
    for initial consultation, 2,
    37
    prepared by paralegals, 43
    requests for production, 62
    review prior to depositions,
    69
    reviewing, 30
    settlement, 19
    settlement conferences, 84
    subpoenas, 62, 146
    for your attorney, 14
domestic support obligations,
    149
domestic violence, 9, 54, 75,
    80, 81, 87, 91, 93, 97, 114

documents, 115
    evidence, 91
domestic violence programs,
    87
    attorney referrals, 87
driver's licenses, 21, 138
drug abuse, 89, 115
dual-income states, 124
duration of the marriage, 141
duress, 6, 185

E
education history, 71, 142
education interruptions, 142
electronics, 16
emergency orders of
    protection, 12, 89, 93
emergency restraining orders,
    2
emergency situations, 87–94
employability, 156
*Employee Retirement Income
    Security Act of 1974
    (ERISA),* 170
employee savings plans, 179
employment records, 119
Equifax, 166
equipment, evaluation, 54
equity in home, 77, 157, 158,
    159
evergreen retainer, 51
evidence, 98, 113, 195, 198,
    201, 204
evidentiary hearing, 127
ex parte court order, 12
exchange date for personal
    property, 16
executive compensation, 180
exhibits, 3, 40, 115, 201, 203,
    204, 212
Experian, 166
expert witnesses, 40, 65, 151,
    162
    fees and costs, 41, 53, 54
    retainer agreement, 54
extracurricular activities, 15,
    37
extramarital relationships, 70,
    106, 143

extraordinary expenses, 15
extraordinary medical
   expenses, 126

F

Facebook, 67
Fair Credit Reporting Act, 166
fair market values, 157
family activities, 25
family businesses, 145
family court, 115, 117
family court judge, 96
family expenses, 146
family law, 32, 81, 110
farm assets, 166
Farm Credit Administration,
   166
farm economics experts, 166
farm operations, 166
federal employee civil service
   retirement benefits, 177
Federal Employees Retirement
   System, 177
Federal Farm Bill, 166
federal pensions, 16
fee agreements, 2, 55
filing fees, 53
filing for divorce, 10, 22
filing status for taxes, 16, 20
financial disclosures, 185
final court hearing, 200
final decree of divorce,
   appealing, 210
final hearings, 196
financial accounts, 2
financial advisor, 75
financial affidavit, 2, 43, 63,
   69, 129
   attachments, 64
   false statements, 63, 64
financial analyses, 40
financial hardships, 128, 193
financial information, 17, 62
   privacy issues, 64
financial institutions,
   subpoena, 146
financial issues, 13, 41, 42, 70,
   139, 212
financial obligations, 140

financial statements, 146
firearms or weapons, 115
fishing license, 138
fixed-term maintenance, 140
flat fees, 49, 50
foreclosures of the home,
   161
forensic accountants, 146,
   166
Form W-4, Employee's
   Withholding Certificate,
   193
formal discovery, 62, 64
former name restoration, 17,
   20, 21
forms and questionnaires, 14
four-way conference, 83
   see also settlement
   conference
*Free Application for Federal
   Student Aid (FAFSA),* 134
free consultations, 33, 48
free legal advice, 47
free legal services, 49
*Freedom of Information Act
   (FOIA),* 166
frequent-flyer miles, 164
friends and family members,
   23, 25, 26, 27, 39, 57, 66,
   113, 159, 196
   in courtroom, 205
full disclosure, 186
furniture, 16
furniture and furnishings, 163
future earning capacity, 140,
   141
future tax consequences, 188

G

gamesmanship, 55, 93
garnishment of wages, 137
gifts and inheritances, 126,
   153, 155
going to court, 38, 40
gross income, 125, 126, 127,
   128, 143, 145, 192
grounds for divorce, 9
guardian *ad litem* (GAL), 41,
   43, 54, 107, 109, 113

advantages, 111
fees and costs, 111
recommendations, 111
role, 110, 111
guns or weapons, 89

H

health care, fees and costs, 171
health history, 142
health insurance, 5, 15, 20, 36, 142, 171, 180
health insurance benefits, 170
hearings, 3, 40, 76, 196
types, 195
HFS child support guidelines, 127, 128, 129
deviations, 126, 128
high-conflict case, 65
homemaker contributions, 156
homemaker responsibilities, 139
household goods, 16, 164
housing market, 159
Hunt Formula, 175
hunting license, 138

I

illegal activities, 70
illegal conduct, 70
Illinois Coalition Against Domestic Violence, 87
Illinois Department of Healthcare and Family Services (HFS), 124, 125, 137, 138
economic tables, 124
online child support calculator, 125
Illinois Marriage and Dissolution of Marriage Act, 139
Illinois Municipal Retirement Fund benefits (IMRF), 178
Illinois State Disbursement Unit, 134, 135
Illinois Supreme Court, 2, 34, 42, 63, 209

Illinois Supreme Court Registration and Disciplinary Commission, 35
Illinois Supreme Court Rules, 19, 38, 40, 62, 79
Illinois Uniform Premarital Agreement Act, 186
Illinois Violence Act of 1986, 98
immigration lawyer, 9
immigration status, 9
in camera interviews, 109
In Re Marriage of Hunt, 175
see also *Hunt Formula,* 175
income information, 76, 124, 129, 135, 140, 141, 142, 156
determining spouse's, 146
undisclosed, 190
income tax, 172, 188
indefinite maintenance, 140
independent financial expert, 41
fees and costs, 41
individualized tax amount, 127
infidelity, 143
informal discovery, 62
informal recommendations, 200
information requests, 40
inheritances, 5, 153, 165
initial consultation, 2, 22, 32, 34, 35, 37, 38, 39, 47, 51, 88
fees and costs, 48
taking children to, 39
injunctions, 13
innocent spouse relief, 190, 193
eligibility requirements, 193
insurance, benefits, 180
insurance policies, 163
intellectual property, 164
interest income, 192
interest rates, 159
interim attorney fees, 13
Internal Revenue Service

Index

(IRS), 190, 193
Internet, 4, 8, 116
  research, 62
interrogatories, 40, 62, 66, 197
  answers to, 69, 203
investments, 16, 163
IRAs (Individual Retirement Accounts), 163, 172, 173, 176
irreconcilable differences, 7, 200
irrevocable special-needs trust, 132
IRS Form 8332, 16, 192
IRS Publication 504, Divorced or Separated Individuals, 188
IRS Publication 523, Selling Your Home, 191
IRS Publication 529, Miscellaneous Deductions, 192

J

job transfers, 119
joint checking accounts, 155
joint credit cards, 167, 168
joint filing status, 190
joint simplified dissolution procedure, 4
joint tax returns, 5, 16, 190, 193
  benefits, 190
  risk factors, 190
journal entries, 115
judge, judges, 3
  changing, 18
judgement for dissolution of marriage, 200
judge's chambers, 196
  see also chambers
judgment of dissolution of marriage, 4, 19, 20
junior lawyers, 50
jurisdiction, 39

K

K-1 stock disclosures, 146
kidnapping, 92, 93, 114

L

law clerks, 43, 44, 55, 58
law research, 203
law schools, 49
law students, 43, 49
Leading Lawyer Network, 33
leases, 164
legal advice, 12
legal arguments, 111
legal assistant, 43
legal documents, 39
legal fees, 47, 60, 77
  borrowing, 49
  charging, 49
  installment payments, 49
legal research, 3, 40, 43, 213
legal secretary, 58
legal separation, 5
legal services, 55
length of marriage, 42, 144, 156
levies against property, 137
liens against personal property, 138
liens against real estate, 138
liens on financial accounts, 138
life insurance, 15, 148, 170, 180, 181
  death benefit, 178, 183
life insurance benefits, 169
lifestyle analysis, 146
like kind exchanges, 153
limited-scope representation, 42, 49
litigation budget, 56, 77
live-in partners, 104
  effect on decision-making rights, 104
  effect on parenting time, 104
livestock, 164
living expenses, 161
LLC interests, 163

M

maintenance, 5, 6, 9, 13, 16, 19, 36, 37, 67, 126, 127, 136, 139–150, 151, 156, 158, 165,

168, 181, 182, 183, 192, 213
calculations, 143, 144
candidates for, 142
changes in circumstances,
149
cohabitation with live-in
partner, 143, 148
death of paying party, 148
death of receiving party,
148
deviation from guidelines,
144
eligibility requirements,
139
enforcement, 149
fixed-term, 140
guidelines, 139, 143, 144
indefinite, 140
information to provide to
attorney, 142
judge's considerations, 140
life insurance to secure, 16
missed payments, 149
modifications, 145, 149
non-modifiable, 148, 150
refusal to pay, 149
remarriage, 148
reserve, 150
reviewable, 140
taxes, 189
temporary, 147
types, 140
undue hardship, 184
waiver, 184, 200
make-up parenting time, 117
malpractice insurance, 35
marital assets, 91, 147
marital balance sheet, 152,
153, 154
marital debts, 165, 167
division, 16
marital home, 2, 13, 77, 93,
156, 157, 189
benefits in keeping, 159
capital gains tax, 191
foreclosure, 160
preparing for sale, 159
refinancing, 158

short sales, 160
tax consequences, 191
tax liabilities, 160
marital property, 91, 140, 152,
163, 164, 173, 178
judge's deciding factors,
156
rules to determine, 153
marital settlement agreement,
19, 36
marital status, 189, 193
marriage counseling, 27
see also counseling
marriage procured by fraud,
6
mediation, 3, 17, 74, 76, 81,
96, 112
benefits, 77
children attendance, 82
failure, 83
mandatory, 79
preparation for, 82
reviewing agreement, 82
role of attorney, 81
shared expense, 82
types of issues, 81
mediators, 37, 40, 74, 76, 79,
81
credentials, 81
fees and costs, 41
training, 81
medical expenses, 37, 126
medical needs, 126
medical records, 58, 66
mental health, 97
mental health professionals,
41
mental health records, 104
mental incapacity, 6
military benefits, 176, 177
survivor benefits, 177
military pensions, 16
misdemeanors, 117
monthly living expenses, 142
monthly statements, 59
mortgages, 129, 157, 159, 160
refinancing, 160
motion to compel, 67

motion to modify
maintenance, 150
motion to reconsider, 208
motions, 12, 129
motivational books, 26
motor vehicles, 16, 163
mutual business evaluator, 84

N

negotiations, 2, 17, 20, 38, 39,
55, 74, 75, 83, 90, 188, 203
benefits, 77
types of issues, 81
nesting arrangement order,
103
net annual income, 143
net income, 126, 127, 143,
144, 145
newspaper publication notice,
8
no-fault divorce, 7
nonmarital assets, 153
nonmarital property, 140, 152,
155
non-qualified retirement
benefits, 179

O

objection in court, 198, 205,
206
occupational certificates, 138
offset against the house, 160
oil and gas royalties, 164
opening statement, 3, 204,
206
opinions, 209
oral arguments, 209, 210
oral motions, 12, 13
order for protection, 88, 89,
90
overtime pay, 126

P

paralegal, 43, 44, 55, 58, 66
fees and costs, 43
parent education classes, 3
parental alienation, 115
parental behavior, 98
parental decision making, 40,
81

parental responsibility, 5, 6,
10, 54, 95–123, 98, 115, 118,
141, 157, 158, 159, 210, 212,
213
parental roles chart, 99, 100
*Parental Kidnapping
Prevention Act (PKPA),* 93
parenting classes, 114
parenting issues, 73, 76, 81,
95, 111, 196
parenting plan, 19, 78, 96,
112
relocation, 118
parenting schedule, 15
parenting times, 12, 13, 24, 37,
40, 54, 70, 81, 83, 88, 89, 97,
98, 99, 102, 103, 104, 106,
107, 111, 112, 114, 116, 117,
119, 120, 124, 171, 192, 210,
213
child reluctance to go, 121
grandparent rights, 123
posting bond, 93
replacement, 119
supervised, 93, 113
parent-teacher conferences,
121
partnerships, 163
passports, 138
patents, 164
*Patient Protection and
Affordable Care Act
(PPACA),* 171
pay stubs, 84
pension plans
administrator, 177
summary plan statements,
180
pensions, 142, 170, 173, 180
survivor benefits, 174
vesting period, 174
perjury, 70
personal finance statements,
146
personal injury lawsuits, 164
personal jurisdiction, 8
personal property division,
16

petition for dissolution of civil unions, 6
petition for dissolution of marriage, 2, 10, 11, 13, 15, 36
petition for legal separation, 5
petition for order to show cause, 136
petitioner, 10, 206
pets, 13, 16, 115, 163
phone conferences, 44
physical health, 26
plaintiff, 206
  witnesses, 206
pleadings, 10, 43, 111, 136
  review prior to depositions, 69
police pensions, 178
police reports, 89
posting bond, 135, 138
postnuptial agreement, 153, 156, 182–187
  challenging, 186
  consultation with attorney, 187
posttrial motion, 207, 210
preliminary injunction, 91
premarital assets, 16
premarital debts, 16
prenuptial agreement, 142, 147, 153, 156, 182–187, 184
  breaking, 183
  child support, 183
  consultation with attorney, 185
  review by attorney, 184
  role of attorney, 184
  subjects covered, 183
  unenforceable criteria, 185
pretrial conference, 85, 199
pretrial motions, 3
primary caregiver, 99
primary home base, 96, 98, 102
prior arrest records, 89
private collection agencies, 138

private court reporters, 202
private income, 141
private investigators, 62, 106
private process server, 2, 11, 12
private retirement funds, 163
privileged communications, 38, 109
pro bono services, 49
pro se representation, 4
probate laws, 5
procedural hearings, 195
procedural issues, 206
process server, 2, 11, 12
professional licenses, 138, 164
professional opportunities, 139
profit-sharing plans, 170, 179
property, 63
  classification, 151, 155
  commingled assets, 153
  date to value, 157
  distribution, 151, 161, 188
  tax consequences, 157
  title to, 152, 155
  valuations, 151, 157
property division, 6, 8, 10, 19, 38
property settlement, 135, 147, 168
property settlement agreement, 157
property valuation, 41
proposals for settlement, 3
protective orders, 64, 88, 89, 103
prove-up hearing, 19, 20, 86, 196, 200
psychologist, 23, 41, 53, 54
public assistance benefits, 126
public income, 141

Q

qualified Illinois domestic relations order (QIDRO), 177
qualified domestic relations

Index

order (QDRO), 16, 19, 172, 173, 175, 178, 200
quarterly estimated tax payments, 193
quitclaim deed, 19

R

real estate, 40, 149, 157, 163
  commissions, 159
  evaluation, 54
  marital expenses, 16
real property, 16
realtor commissions, 160
rebuttal witnesses, 207
reconciliation, 7, 27
recreational vehicles, 16
re-direct examination, 207
referrals, 2
refreshing your recollection, 198
relocation, 118, 142, 213
  benefits to children, 119
  reason for move, 119
remarriage, 5, 136
removal of children from home, 9
removal of children from state, 2
rentals, 16
replacement parenting time, 119
requests for admissions of fact or genuineness of documents, 62
requests for information, 25
requests for production of documents, 40, 62, 66
reserve maintenance, 150
residency requirements, 7, 8, 9
respondent, 10, 206
responses to motions, 13
restraining orders, 13, 14, 89, 90, 105
restricted stock, 170
restricted stock units (RSUs), 179, 180
  vesting period, 179
retainer, 2, 48, 50, 51, 56

additional, 51
evergreen, 51
monthly payments, 51
refunding unused, 52
retirement benefits, 19, 38, 126, 163, 169, 180
retirement income, 141
retirement plans, 5, 16, 36, 135
reviewable maintenance, 140
reviewing monthly billing statements, 53
RSU benefits, 16
rules of evidence, 83

S

safety concerns, 88
safety plan, 87
school counselors, 24
school events, 120
scope of representation, 52
self-employment, 135, 145
separate credit, 166
separation, 5
settlement agreements, 3, 19, 36, 74, 200
settlement conferences, 3, 29, 39, 40, 83, 84, 199
  judge's opinion, 85
  preparation for, 84
  procedure, 84
  role of attorney, 85
settlement negotiations, 56, 78, 204
sex offender, 98
sexual intercourse, 6
sexual orientation, 107
shared parenting schedule, 130
sheriff, 2, 11, 12, 137
shotgun weddings, 6
shuttle negotiations, 29
simple IRA, 16
social media, 26, 67
  deleting accounts, 67
Social Security Act, 170
Social Security Administration (SSA), 131
Social Security benefits, 5,

126, 169, 180
Social Security disability
    benefits, 131
Social Security profile, 21
social service resources, 133
social workers, 113
speaking to attorney in court,
    202
spiritual advisors, 27
split residences, 102
spoliation of evidence, 67
spousal support,
    see maintenance
stalking, 98
standard of living, 141, 142
standardized tax amount, 127
state statutes, 4, 52, 117, 124
state tax refunds, 138
State Universities Retirement
    System (SURS), 178
Statement of Client's Rights
    and Responsibilities, 52
state's attorney, 137
status hearings, 195
stock options, 16, 163, 170,
    178, 179
    taxes, 179
stress, 79
student loans, 165
subpoenas, 58, 65, 146
    blocking, 67
    of documents, 62
    employers, 180
    fees and costs, 53
    financial institutions, 67
    medical records, 66
    spouse's employer, 67
substantive hearings, 195,
    196
suicide threats, 115
summary hearing, 127
summons, 90
Super Lawyer, 33
Supplemental Nutrition
    Assistance Program (SNAP),
    126
support groups, 24, 26
support orders, 14

support withholding orders,
    135, 200
surviving spouse benefits,
    178
sworn testimony, 68

T

tax advisors, 190, 193
tax attorney, 190
tax deductions, 143
tax evasion, 190
tax exemptions for children,
    15
tax filing status, 189
tax issues, 189
tax law, 193
tax liabilities, 173, 190, 191
tax planning, 190
tax refunds, 138
tax returns, 2, 16, 25, 37, 58,
    84, 128, 145
taxes, 36, 127, 145, 157, 176,
    178, 188–193
    marital status, 189
    withholding from wages,
    190
Teachers' Retirement System
    benefits (TRS), 178
temporary assistance benefits,
    126
temporary child support, 13
temporary hearing, 12, 13,
    103, 199
    issues decided at, 13
temporary order, 13, 14, 16
    appealing, 210
temporary parenting issues, 2
temporary parenting orders,
    103
temporary parenting time,
    199
temporary restraining orders
    (TRO), 11, 166
temporary support, 2, 199
temporary support hearings,
    129
testifying as witness, 205
testimony in court, 198
testimony of witnesses, 97,

Index

199
preservation, 69
use of notes during, 198
text messages, 67
therapists, 23, 26, 27, 41, 104
threatening letters, e-mails,
voicemails, 97
time-shares, 16
tools, 16
tools or equipment, 163
trademarks, 164
traditional attorney, 111
transcripts of court
proceeding, 202, 213
transcripts of testimony, 62
TransUnion, 166
trial, going to trial, 3, 54, 69,
77, 78, 124, 188, 194–208,
212
fees and costs, 56
preparation for, 198, 203
speaking to attorney in
court, 202
steps, 206
trial assistant, 43
trial dates, 3, 76, 80, 204
trial exhibits, 212
trial notebook, 204
trial preparation, 3, 203
trial retainer, 56
tribal court, 9
trusts, 183
turnover orders, 137

U

unconscionable agreements,
19, 186
undue hardship, 147
unemployment compensation,
135
*Uniform Child Custody
Jurisdiction Enforcement Act
(UCCJEA)*, 93
University of Illinois in
Urbana-Champaign, 134
Unlawful Visitation or
Parenting Time Interference,
117
U.S. Department of Labor,

171
U.S. Department of State, 92
Children's Passport Issuance
Alert Program, 92

V

variable income, 128
Violence Against Women Act,
9
visitation, 101
see parental responsibility,
parenting time
vocational skills, 156

W

W-2s, 146
wages, 145
waiting period, 9, 10
waivers, 150
warrants, 137
wills, 183
withholding allowances, 193
witness impeachment, 69
witness stand, 109, 194, 197,
201
witnesses, 3, 40, 61, 68, 107,
108, 199, 202, 203, 204, 205,
206
credibility, 70, 108
cross-examination, 3
depositions, 204
direct examination, 3
discrediting, 63
forcing testimony, 109
interviewing, 43, 62, 204
reluctant, 109
subpoenas, 3, 109
testimony, 65, 199
work history, 71, 142
work schedules, 101
worker's compensation, 135,
164
working with attorney, 32–46
written closing arguments,
207
written fee agreements, 47,
52
written interrogatories, 40
written motions, 12
written parenting plan, 19

About the Author

Steven N. Peskind, Esq., is the principal of Peskind Law Firm, which represents clients throughout the State of Illinois. Mr. Peskind is a fellow of the American Academy of Matrimonial Lawyers and the International Academy of Family Lawyers. In 2015 he was elected as a diplomate of the American College of Family Trial Lawyers, which is limited to the top 100 family law trial lawyers from across the United States. Diplomates are chosen based upon their recognized litigation skills and courtroom abilities. Mr. Peskind serves on the faculty of the Family Law Trial Advocacy Institute, presented annually in Boulder, Colorado.

He has published five family law–related books, including his most recent, *A Practitioners Guide to the Illinois Marriage and Dissolution of Marriage Act and the Illinois Parentage Act,* published by IICLE in 2017. He has been designated an Illinois Super Lawyer and is a member of the Leading Lawyer's Network. In 2015 Best Lawyers honored Mr. Peskind by designating him as family lawyer of the year in Chicago.

Divorce Titles from Addicus Books

Visit our online catalog at www.AddicusBooks.com

Divorce in Alabama: The Legal Process, Your Rights, and What to Expect $21.95

Divorce in Arizona: The Legal Process, Your Rights, and What to Expect. $21.95

Divorce in California: The Legal Process, Your Rights, and What to Expect $21.95

Divorce in Connecticut: The Legal Process, Your Rights, and What to Expect $21.95

Divorce in Florida: The Legal Process, Your Rights, and What to Expect $21.95

Divorce in Georgia: Simple Answers to Your Legal Questions $21.95

Divorce in Idaho: The Legal Process, Your Rights, and What to Expect. $21.95

Divorce in Illinois: The Legal Process, Your Rights, and What to Expect—2nd Edition. $21.95

Divorce in Kansas: The Legal Process, Your Rights, and What to Expect $21.95

Divorce in Louisiana: The Legal Process, Your Rights, and What to Expect $21.95

Divorce in Maine: The Legal Process, Your Rights, and What to Expect $21.95

Divorce in Maryland: The Legal Process, Your Rights, and What to Expect $21.95

Divorce in Michigan: The Legal Process, Your Rights, and What to Expect. $21.95

Divorce in Mississippi: The Legal Process, Your Rights, and What to Expect. $21.95

A Guide to Divorce in Missouri: Simple Answers to Complex Questions $21.95

Divorce in Nebraska: The Legal Process, Your Rights, and What to Expect—2nd Edition $21.95

Divorce in Nevada: The Legal Process, Your Rights, and What to Expect. $21.95

Divorce in New Jersey: The Legal Process, Your Rights, and What to Expect $21.95

Divorce in New York: The Legal Process, Your Rights, and What to Expect $21.95

Divorce in North Carolina: The Legal Process, Your Rights, and What to Expect $21.95

Divorce in Oklahoma: The Legal Process, Your Rights, and What to Expect $21.95

Divorce in Pennsylvania: The Legal Process, Your Rights, and What to Expect $21.95

Divorce in South Carolina: The Legal Process, Your Rights, and What to Expect $21.95

Divorce in Tennessee: The Legal Process, Your Rights, and What to Expect $21.95

Divorce in Texas: The Legal Process, Your Rights, and What to Expect $21.95

Divorce in Virginia: The Legal Process, Your Rights, and What to Expect $21.95

Divorce in Washington: The Legal Process, Your Rights, and What to Expect $21.95

Divorce in West Virginia: The Legal Process, Your Rights, and What to Expect $21.95

Divorce in Wisconsin: The Legal Process, Your Rights, and What to Expect $21.95

Daily Meditations for Healing from Divorce: Discovering the New You. $21.95

To order books from Addicus Books:

Please send:

_____ copies of _____
(Title of book)

at $ _____ each   TOTAL _____

NE residents add 6% sales tax   _____

Add Shipping
$6.75 for first book
$1.10 for each additional book   _____

TOTAL ENCLOSED   _____

Name _____

Address _____

City _____ State _____ Zip _____

☐ Visa   ☐ Mastercard   ☐ AMEX   ☐ Discover

Credit card number _____

Expiration date _____

Three digit CVV number on back of card _____

Order by credit card or personal check.

To Order Books:
Visit us online at: www.AddicusBooks.com
Call toll free: (800) 888-4741

 Addicus Books
P. O. Box 45327
Omaha, NE 68145